I0469920

BANKS

AND

THE MULTIPLIER EFFECT
OF MONEY

SKIP ANDREWS

ISBN: 1481863738
ISBN-13: 9781481863735

To my children,
their spouses, and my children's children.

TABLE OF CONTENTS

INTRODUCTION

Economics is about money; that is the bottom line. The key to understanding the science of economics is to understand money. The key to understanding money is to understand banks. If you don't understand money and banks, chances are you will never really grasp economic theory.

If politicians don't understand money and economics, how can they create laws and regulations that will allow the financial and economic markets to work as they ought to? If we don't understand economics and money, how can we elect representatives who know what they are doing, as well as hold their feet to the fire if they don't do their jobs right?

It took me many years to figure out some of the things I am explaining in this book simply because I wasn't taught all of these things in college as a business student and had to learn them on my own. I will attempt to explain what is going on as carefully and precisely as I can. Of course money and banks can't be separated, so a lot will be said about how banks function and use money.

Every area of human endeavor has its own particular words and phrases, or jargon, as it is sometimes called; explanations of money and banking thus require using proper economic terminology. Where words are unclear, I will try to rephrase them in language that is simpler or more commonly understood. I will also use small, simplified balance sheets to illustrate what happens to the money at each step. The written words have to be taken in by the mind and assimilated in a way that we can understand them. The balance sheets are a visual representation of what is written—for those who are visual learners.

I should also state that I believe banks offer many great and important services, and it is not my intent to imply that we should do away with banks. On the other hand, many individuals, as they read this book, may feel justified in their beliefs that banks are nothing short of evil and should therefore be done away with or otherwise regulated into impotency. The individual is free to determine how he or she feels about the facts and can, with reason, choose to react positively or negatively to banks and their working policies. My intention is to explain the system as best as I can with the hope that once you know how the multiplier effect of money works, and its attendant consequences, you will be able to make rational decisions about what ought to be done or not done in relation to the system and how you can use the system to your own benefit.

PART 1

To begin with we will look at the multiplier effect of money and how money is multiplied.

Extremes are only dangerous when
we think there is nothing else!

LOOKING AT THE EXTREME

In trying to understand how the world works, it is often advisable to take out all but one variable and take what is finally left to the extreme. In the extreme it becomes apparent what the outcomes are and the changes that caused them, as well as how the changes influence the whole process we are studying. Take inflation. The opposite of inflation is deflation. If you were to plot inflation and deflation on a continuum, it would look like this, with runaway inflation at one end and severe deflation at the opposite end:

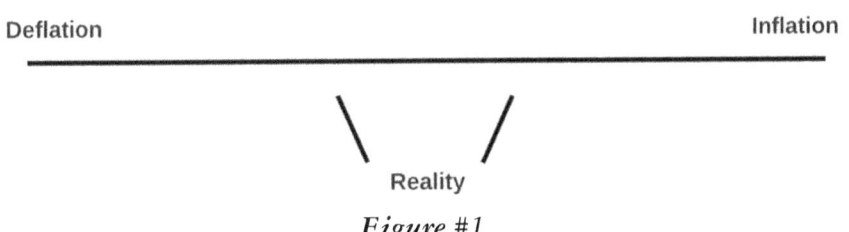

Figure #1

When we look at the real world, things don't usually function at either extreme end of the continuum. Generally the world is much more centered between the two extremes, and that is why I have labeled the center of the continuum as reality. The world is much more centrist because there are multiple factors involved, usually a plethora of factors, that influence inflation and deflation. Some of the factors are deflationary, and some are inflationary, so they tend to cancel each other out—or at least partially cancel each other out. So reality ends up in the middle somewhere. If, on the other hand, we eliminate all but one of the factors and then push the analysis of that factor to the extreme, it is much easier to see what the effects of a single stimulus can be.

Human beings want to simplify things so they only have to deal with one cause and effect at a time. If there are many factors involved, it is simply too complex for most humans to deal with and requires much more than a sound bite to explain what is going on. Besides that, it is difficult to get emotional and uptight about something that requires a lengthy explanation. It seems that in this day and age, if it can't be explained in a sound bite, it didn't happen, doesn't exist, or is simply ignored with the hope that it will go away. Politicians are really good at simplifying things to one cause and one effect. Usually the cause is the other party or, at the very least, the other political contestant, and the effect is a disaster at the opposite extreme from the position he or she espouses, which makes it really easy to get pumped up about. In general the desire to simplify and accuse someone else seems to be human nature. In the end I hope to keep things simple and straightforward without prejudicing you against what is explained.

In this book I will do a lot of simplifying and looking at extremes for the sake of explaining basic ideas. Don't get hung up on the idea that something is oversimplified or extreme or that I am trying to pin all the blame on banks. Reality really is more centrist. The extreme merely serves to show how one factor can affect the basic idea. All the other factors involved will either exacerbate or minimize the effect we are looking at. The important thing to remember is to understand the concept being explained and what the expected consequences are or should be from a change in one factor. Once a concept is understood, you may add any other factors you might choose and make a much more complex version with your own analysis. But first, understand the basics.

Armed with the concepts of what is really happening in the world of banking and money, you can draw your own conclusions and make your own decisions about what is right and what is not. Meanwhile I hope you enjoy the read.

Economics is often termed the "dismal science."
Perhaps it is dismal because at times it seems so foreign
to our common everyday lives that it is tedious and meaningless.

TWO FRIENDS AND A FATHER

While trying to recruit several friends for my campaign committee, I had the hope of running for President of the United States; I invariably got into a discussion with them about some of the current issues. One of the hottest issues back then was the financial crisis and problems stemming from it.

One day I approached Ed (not his real name) at his home, where I happened to be working. We got on the subject of the issues and eventually entertained ourselves with the financial crisis. We got into the dealings of the banks and overnight loans. In the early days of the financial crisis, almost no bank was willing to do overnight loans, so the banks were at a standstill and could do almost nothing that banks normally did. Without overnight loans they were basically belly-up and dead in the water. Fortunately the Federal Reserve and other central banks can provide overnight loans, and after realizing what had happened, the central banks saved the day. After discussing overnight loans, I mentioned that banks created money out of thin air, and Ed went over the edge.

Eventually I was able to ask him if he knew how banks made money, as in profit. His answer was that they made it through interest on loans and through fees of a wide variety. I pointed out that banks did indeed make money off of interest and fees, but these were not the primary ways that banks made money. Well, he was beginning to think I was a few fries short of a Happy Meal.

I asked Ed if he understood what the multiplier effect of money was, and he said that he did. I pointed out that the bank only has to keep 10% of the cash it receives from deposits, and it will loan out the other 90% to other people, and by doing this the bank can multiply the money in the system by another nine times, thus creating money out of thin air. Please understand that I was going on the assumption that he did indeed understand the multiplier effect of money, so what I said to him was by no means a complete or detailed explanation of the multiplier effect. I will get to that in the following chapter.

Ed pointed out to me that if you were to look at a bank's books, all the money would be accounted for and backed by loans or other assets or financial instruments, so it was definitely not creating money out of thin air. Of course what he said about the banks' financial statements is true, and I found myself up against a brick wall. I changed my tack and tried to explain the multiplier effect in terms of leverage. We were still definitely not on the same page, and, in the ensuing confusion, I botched my explanation of leverage as it pertains to the multiplier effect. Now I was up against a rock and talking to a brick wall while still trying to convince Ed that banks really did create money out of thin air. Later I went over the classic definition of the multiplier effect of money with him, and he agreed that banks do indeed create money, but I was left with the feeling that he was really humoring me to some extent and didn't really understand the full import of the multiplier effect of money.

That is one story. The other story is about a friend of mine I shall call Michael. He and I were traveling home together from St.

Louis with lots of time to kill. Michael was trained as an economist and had worked in the investment department of a major bank. So we tackled the financial crisis as well as other political issues. He clearly understood the multiplier effect but understood it in an entirely different way than I did. He didn't give any credit to the idea of banks creating money out of thin air. I tried using leverage as an explanation, but his experience in dealing with investments at the bank where he had worked involved the concept of borrowing money at a low rate of interest and then loaning the same money out at a higher rate. The difference between the interest rate at which you borrowed and the interest rate at which you loaned out the money was leveraging your money. But that is not what the multiplier effect is all about. He couldn't grasp that borrowing money and then loaning the same money out to someone else doesn't multiply money, as in the multiplier effect of money—it merely shuffles money around.

The first story is about Ed. He is not only a friend but also a successful businessman, entrepreneur, and investor who invests in startups or expanding businesses. He is very intelligent, hardworking, outgoing, and just a great guy for whom I have a great deal of respect. However, he just didn't get it.

The second individual, Michael, is also a friend and is a leader in my church at the local level. In my church there is no paid ministry, so he has always worked for a living in the business community. While trained as an economist and having worked for a large bank for a number of years, he is now in marketing. He is confident, energetic, diligent, and intelligent. I also have a great deal of respect for him, but once again, like my friend Ed, he just didn't get it.

The bottom line of these two stories is that my friends just didn't get it. They didn't understand the multiplier effect of money. The other side of the coin is that I was unable to explain the multiplier effect to them in such a way that they could understand it.

My parents divorced before I was old enough to remember my father, and over the years we didn't communicate much, until after I was a father myself. As of late we have communicated much more, and for the most part I think we are both grateful for the change as well as for the things we have learned about each other. During the financial crisis in 2008, my father called, and we started talking about the financial state of the country. We got on the subject of the cause of the financial crisis and banks and how they operate. I ventured a very brief explanation of the multiplier effect of money and what part it played in the crisis. When I was done with my spiel, my father agreed and made the comment that at least 95% of all the people in this country didn't understand the principles I had mentioned. I was both shocked and somewhat delighted by his comments.

My father grew up on a farm in rural Virginia. At the age of eighteen, he dropped out of college and went into the military. He wanted to fly more than anything in this world, and the war offered him the opportunity to become a pilot. He joined the war effort in Europe, flying a B-29. After he returned to the States, he received degrees in both psychology and electrical engineering. He then entered a career that made him an engineer and scientist. As a youth he loved reading and became a natural speed reader. In junior high school, he set a goal to read every book in the school library by the time he left junior high. He accomplished his goal before the end of his first school year. He also claims he had a near-photographic memory. He has always been a voracious reader, and I suppose somewhere in all his reading he had picked up the concept of the multiplier effect of money and how banks work.

Based on experiences such as these, I felt the need to write a book that would hopefully be of help to the majority of the people who have no concept of the multiplier effect and how banks function. In the next chapter, I will jump right into the multiplier effect, and in the subsequent chapters, I will explain how it applies in the real world, as well as the not so obvious results that come from it all.

If you have never learned that money can get out of hand,
you simply don't live on the same planet that I do.
But multiplying money?
Really?

THE MULTIPLIER EFFECT
OF MONEY

I think it was Econ 105, an introduction to macroeconomics, where I first learned about the multiplier effect of money. It was my first economics class and my introduction to the school of business. It was simple enough for me to understand the concept, but it had no meaning for me as a young student beyond the textbook explanation. It wasn't until years later that I learned through reading that I really—as well as the people I was reading—was missing some pieces of the puzzle. Eventually I ended up talking to someone at the Federal Reserve Bank in Kansas City. Since I live on the edge of Kansas City, the Tenth District Federal Reserve Bank was an easy target, and with its help, things started coming together.

I should also say, before I go much further, that the normal operations of banks are not only legal but also regulated to a certain point. Banks and the services they offer to the public and businesses are absolutely indispensable. I hope no one will think I am in any way proposing that banks should be abolished or that they are inherently evil. Reality dictates that they are not only indispensable but they also can indeed wreak havoc and therefore need some regulation. Being educated sufficiently to understand banks and what they do is a prerequisite to living with a good system and keeping it from going awry.

I suppose to be not only clear but also intrepid, I need to define several terms and practices that apply to the banking system and its regulation, or you may be lost from the start. The first is the **Federal Reserve Bank or FRB.** *The FRB is really The Federal Reserve System* and is comprised of the District banks and the Board of governors. Both have separate duties but as we refer to the Federal Reserve Bank we are often referring to functions of both at the same time. When referring to the general system or to multiple roles or multiple district banks I will use the term *Federal Reserve*. If I need to refer to one area and its specific functions I will designate it appropriately. In its normal everyday mode, the Federal Reserve is a clearinghouse for all money exchanges between banks. If you write a check at the grocery store, the grocery store deposits your check in its bank. The grocery stores bank then sends the check to the Federal Reserve. The Federal Reserve sends the check to your bank, which keeps your check and sends the money from your account to the Federal Reserve, who in turn forwards the money to the grocery store's bank, and its bank puts the money in the grocery store's account. In recent years this process has been streamlined by the use of digital means, but it still accomplishes the same thing. The Federal Reserve keeps immaculate records of all this money and its travels. The Federal Reserve also regulates all those banks to some extent. It also has many other functions that I won't explain here, but you should understand its clearinghouse and regulatory status.

The second term we need to understand is the *reserve requirement*. The Federal Reserve requires banks to keep on hand at all times one-tenth of all demand deposits in their vaults or in the vaults of the Federal Reserve. This is regulation. This 10% must be in cash—not checks, not securities, or even gold. It is cash only; and yes, this is an important concept to know, so don't lose it because you will need it later on.

Demand deposits are deposits that you have made at the bank, savings or checking of any variety, for which you can walk into the bank and withdraw that money, on demand, in cash. Of course if you can walk into the bank and withdraw the money, you can also achieve the same thing with a check or debit card or e-payment. In the case of checks, debit cards, and e-payments, someone else demands payment from your account—hopefully you already understand this.

Balance sheets are another concept you ought to understand, but first we must have an example to put on the balance sheet to see how it works.

So let's create a situation and its balance sheet!

The multiplier effect of money is best explained in terms of you. Suppose you receive $1,000.00 on payday from your employer *in cash* and promptly deposit the money in your bank account. Your bank has to keep 10% of your money in its vault in cash. This is what the *reserve requirement* is about. The bank will loan the other 90% of your deposit to someone else. The bank now has $100.00 in cash in its vaults and a mortgage or lien on some property with a value of $900.00. The person who got the $900.00 loan deposits it in his account. When the $900.00 ends up in someone's bank account at his or her bank, his or her bank keeps 10% of that person's deposit in its vault and loans out $810.00 (90% of $900.00) to someone else. The recipient of the $810.00 loan deposits his money in his bank, and the process starts all over again. The value of each succeeding loan gets smaller until there is nothing left to loan.

Now look at the big picture. We have created $10,000.00 in demand deposits (your original $1,000.00 + $900.00 + $810.00 + $729.00…). We have also created $1,000.00 in reserves [$100.00 (of your original deposit of $1,000.00) + $90.00 + $81.00 + $72.90…]. We have also created $9,000.00 in loans ($900.00 + $810.00 + $729.00…). This has been a long diatribe about the $900.00 (of your $1,000.00 deposit) and how it was multiplied into more money, but you must understand how it happens.

The bottom line is we have taken your $1,000.00 and turned it into $10,000.00. That means we have multiplied your money ten times. If the reserve requirement had been 20%, we would have multiplied your $1,000.00 by 5 (20% is one-fifth of 100%, so you would multiply the reserve requirement by 5), and we would have ended up with $5,000.00 in demand deposits. If the reserve requirement had been 5%, you would have ended up with $20,000.00 in demand deposits (5% is one-twentieth of 100%, so you would multiply by 20).

This is the multiplier effect of money. Simply stated it is the amount of cash in the system times the inverse of the reserve requirement. 10/1, or 10, is the inverse of one-tenth (1/10). This means that, in the big picture, if there were $1,000.00 in cash in the US economy, or banking system, people would be using (spending) $10,000.00 in money. Of course $1,000.00 would be in cash, and the other $9,000.00 would be on paper (on the books) only. The $9,000.00 does not exist anywhere in the form of paper bills or coins. It only exists in the accounting ledgers of the banks. In Econ 105 they didn't explain the part about it being on the books only. You should understand, though, that there is $10,000.00 in demand deposits in the various banks, and people are spending that $10,000.00 as fast as they can. We have indeed created $9,000.00 out of thin air. It didn't exist before, and the cash still doesn't exist, but people are spending it. The money is there but only on the books.

We have created a situation using a deposit you have made at your bank and followed it through the process of the multiplier effect, so now let us look at the balance sheet associated with the process. In reality we have created the scenario for three bank balance sheets: two for your bank and another that is a composite balance sheet for your bank plus all the other banks where all those loans were deposited.

Your bank's balance sheets would look like these:

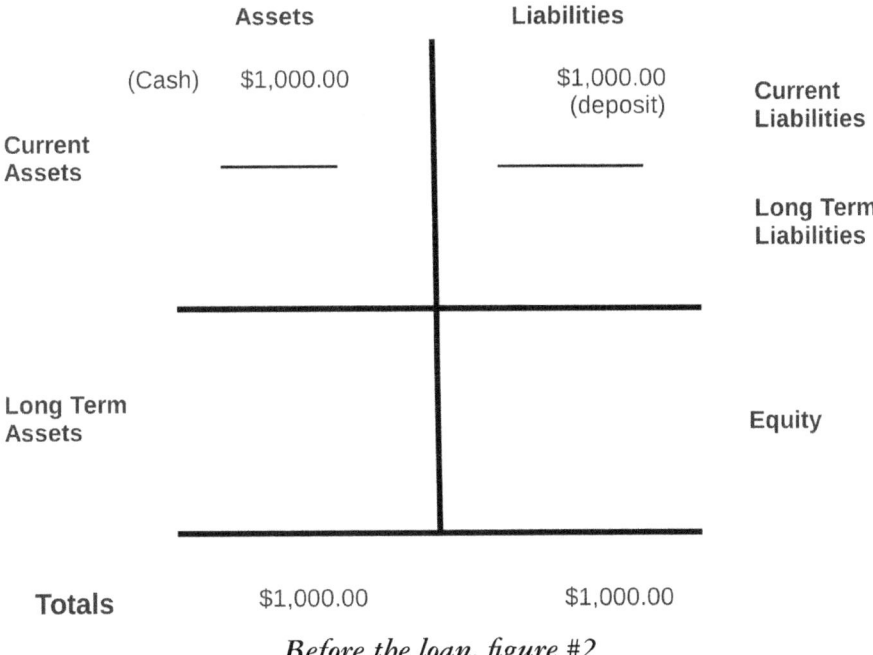

Before the loan, figure #2

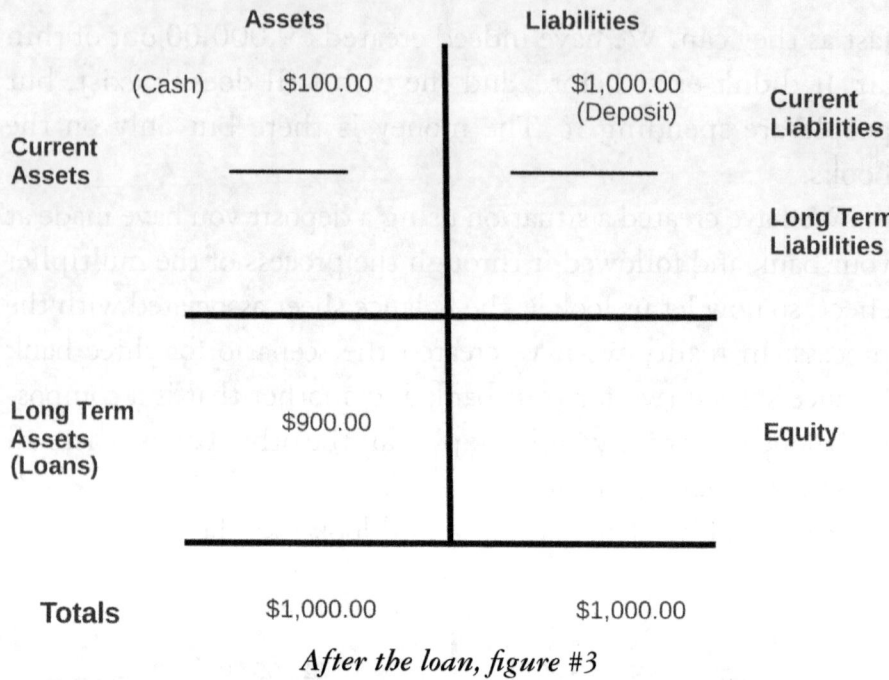

After the loan, figure #3

You will also notice that both balance sheets, one after the deposit but before the loan and the other after the loan, have the same totals at the bottom. No extra money has been created. In the next diagram, figure 4, we see the effect of all the loans and deposits from the various banks. It clearly shows that there has been money created.

Now here comes the explanation of a *balance sheet*. A *balance sheet* has two sides (columns) with a line drawn down the middle. On the left are the *assets* or things the bank owns. On the right are the *sources* of the money that the bank used to buy the assets in the left-hand column. Another way of looking at the balance sheet is to say that on the left is what the bank owns and on the right is who "really" owns those assets.

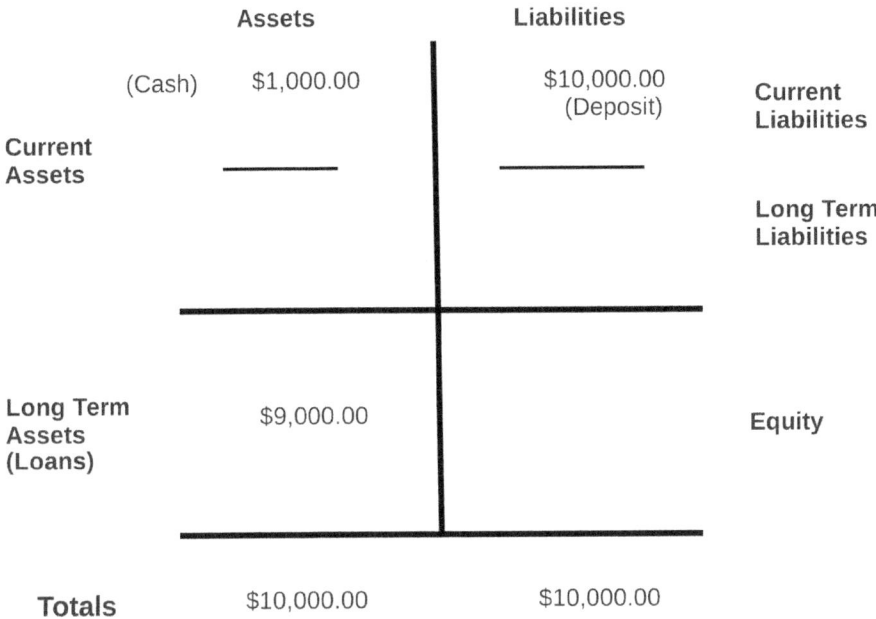

The composite balance sheet would look like this, figure 4

In the first example, you deposited $1,000.00, and since it is your money, not the bank's, it is entered on the right side as if it were a loan the bank had taken from you, which in reality it is. Most people don't think of it as a loan, probably because they don't get any interest for depositing their paycheck in the bank, plus it is still yours to spend. The bank now has $1,000.00 in cash, so it lists the cash as an asset under cash on the left side of the balance sheet.

You will notice that there are totals at the bottom of each column. The two totals, left and right columns, must always be equal. The dollar amount of assets you own (left side) and the money you had to buy them with (right side) is always the same, in dollar amounts, on a balance sheet.

In the second illustration, we further divide the asset column (left side) of the balance sheet into two parts. One part is cash or securities that are the equivalent of cash. If you can sell a security immediately and be paid for it today, that security is considered to be cash or as good as cash. The second or lower division on the left side of the balance sheet is for long-term assets. Since the $900.00 loan the bank made won't be paid off for two or more years and is not easily turned into cash on the spur of the moment, it is therefore considered a long-term asset, so the loan goes under long-term assets.

On the right side of the balance sheet, the column is also divided into two sections. The top section is for loans of various kinds, which demand deposits are considered to be. The bottom section in the right-hand column is reserved for equity. Equity is the part of the money used to pay for the assets that the bank actually owns. It is the bank's money, not money obtained from loans or deposits. Equity usually consists of money from stock the bank has issued or from profits. At this point we are going to say the bank has $1,000.00 in equity and leave a further explanation of equity for later. Equity is an important part of the balance sheet, so we will add it now, but in the classical explanation of the multiplier effect of money, equity is not mentioned, so we will talk about equity later when it comes into play. At the same time, we have to add the $1,000.00 to the left side of the balance sheet. We will assume the bank used the $1,000.00 to buy stock on the stock market, which would be listed along with cash. The new balance sheet with equity would look like Figure 5.

Again, if you add up everything in the left-hand column and total it and then add up everything in the right-hand column, the two totals at the bottom should be identical. The bottom line on a balance sheet is supposed to be balanced, one side the

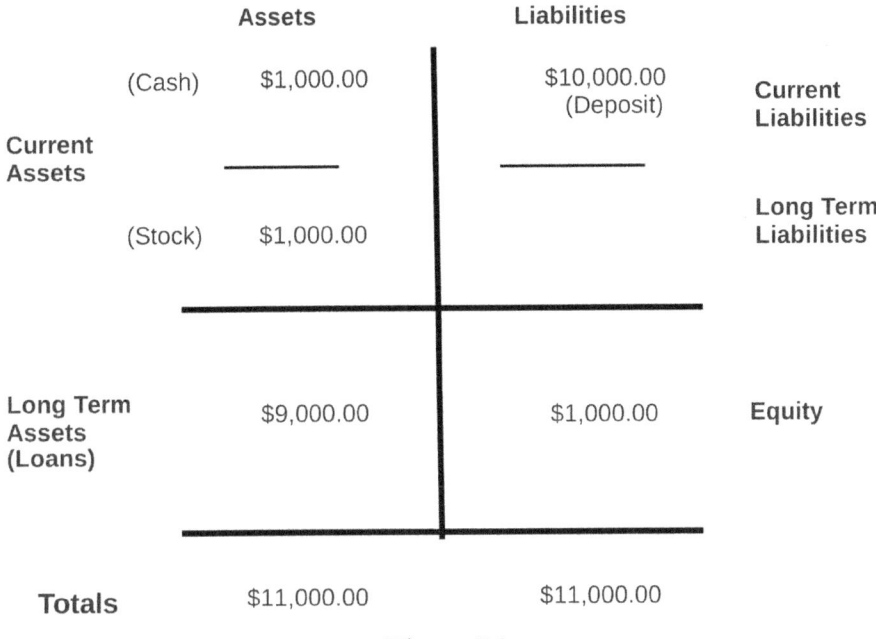

	Assets	Liabilities	
(Cash)	$1,000.00	$10,000.00 (Deposit)	Current Liabilities
Current Assets	————	————	
			Long Term Liabilities
(Stock)	$1,000.00		
Long Term Assets (Loans)	$9,000.00	$1,000.00	Equity
Totals	$11,000.00	$11,000.00	

Figure #5

same as the other side; that is why it is called a balance sheet. Of course if things don't add up to the same amount on both sides of the balance sheet, the regulators and the IRS start asking tough questions, and the accountant usually gets fired.

Going back to the balance sheet in figure 4 before adding equity, the composite balance sheet gives a view of what all the banks have done as your $1,000.00 is loaned out and redeposited in a series of banks. The $900.00 loaned creates a series of deposits and loans, and the resulting total looks like the balance sheet in figure 4. We now have $10,000.00 in deposits, $1,000.00 in cash, and $9,000.00 in loans. Each column now adds up to $10,000.00. In all the banks concerned, we have $1,000.00 in cash and $9,000.00 in new money, which is really only on the books. Even though the bank loaned out $900.00 of your cash, it still claims you have your $1,000.00 in cash in your account.

The second bank still claims that the $900.00 deposited in its customer's account is actually in the customer's account even though the bank loaned out $810.00 of it. In reality there is only your $1,000.00 in the system, and the other $9,000.00 really is created out of thin air. It wasn't there before, but now it is. It is not in the form of currency and only exists on paper (on the books). The extra money is created through the series of loans and deposits that happened at the other banks.

This is the multiplier effect of money explained, and I hope I have done a proper job so you understand it. Every university student who takes a beginning macroeconomics class has to learn this definition, minus the part about the money being created out of thin air and the accompanying balance sheets. Of course I'm repeating myself, but you must understand the principle and how it works, or the rest of this book will be pointless.

Out of thin air? Really?
It didn't exist before
But now it does,
and the balance sheet balances!

THE NOT SO THIN AIR

One can claim that banks are creating money out of thin air because money is created. The money didn't exist before but is here and being used because it has been deposited into the accounts of individuals, businesses, and governments. All this makes it appear as if it came out of thin air.

If you look at the description of how the multiplier effect works, which was presented in the last chapter, it is apparent that the banks created not only an extra $9,000.00 in demand deposits but also an equal amount of loans. These loans are generally backed by some kind of security, which means the money was borrowed from the bank to buy an asset. An asset can be a car, furniture, a house, a building, or equipment. The bank will actually hold ownership of the asset through a mortgage or lien until the loan is paid off. So the bank has exchanged 90% of your demand deposit for a loan that has an asset to back the loan in case the borrower defaults. If you look at the two balance sheets for your bank once more, they show that no extra money has been created. The money simply moved from cash to the long-term assets part of the left hand column of the balance sheet.

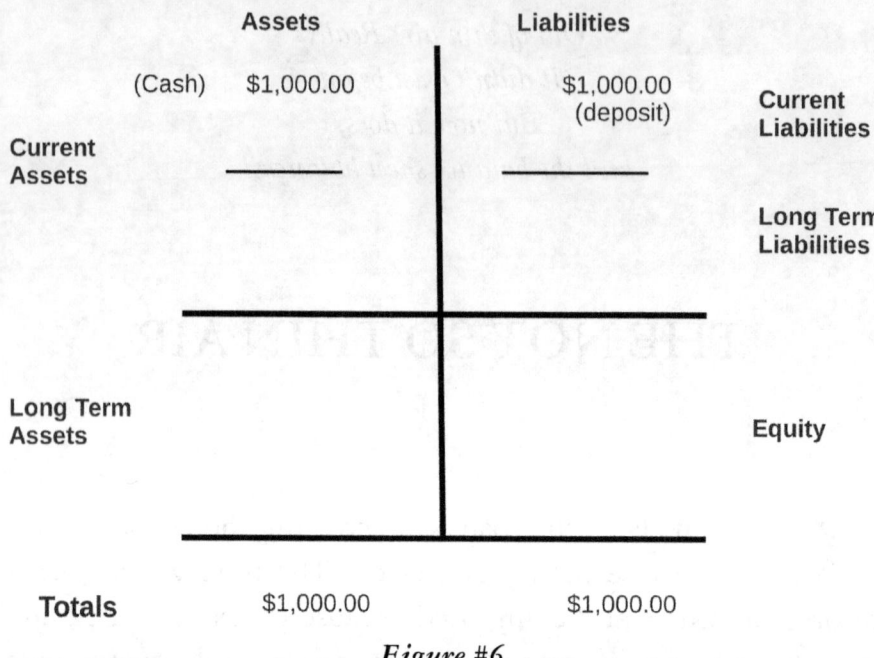

	Assets		Liabilities	
(Cash)	$1,000.00		$1,000.00 (deposit)	Current Liabilities
Current Assets	———		———	
				Long Term Liabilities
Long Term Assets				Equity
Totals	$1,000.00		$1,000.00	

Figure #6

	Assets		Liabilities	
(Cash)	$100.00		$1,000.00 (Deposit)	Current Liabilities
Current Assets	———		———	
				Long Term Liabilities
Long Term Assets (Loans)	$900.00			Equity
Totals	$1,000.00		$1,000.00	

Figure #7

22

It is noteworthy that banks can make unsecured loans. Of course this means that there is no collateral to back the loan. An unsecured loan is usually considered very risky. Governments and large corporations can borrow money by selling bonds to banks or investors, and these bonds are often unsecured. Both big corporations and governments can be so big that they are believed incapable of failing. General Motors and Greece are simply too big to fail; however, in general, unsecured bonds issued by governments and large corporations have been looked on favorably by investors and have for the most part been reliable and stable investments. Bond rating agencies also provide banks and investors with a grading system that tells the buyers how safe the bonds are—or at least that is the idea. Banks, like private investors, are free to invest or make loans in the form of bonds

I just showed on the balance sheet that no extra money had been created. The creation of the money, due to the multiplier effect, happens when the money that is handed out through the loan shows up in someone else's bank account. When I showed you the composite balance sheet of all the loans and deposits created because of your deposit, it was obvious that the money had indeed been created.

In the traditional tale of how the multiplier effect works, the money loaned out ends up in a deposit in a different bank. But suppose for a minute that the money ended up being deposited at the same bank from which it originated. In fact let's assume that each succeeding loan right on down the chain of loans ended up in the same bank. When you take out a business loan, the bank usually asks that you open an account there if you don't already have one so the money really does go back into demand deposits at the same bank, whereas a home loan might go to a contractor who deals with another bank. Again, using your

$1,000.00 as an example and assuming that all the loans created down the line remained at your bank, the balance sheet for your bank would look like this:

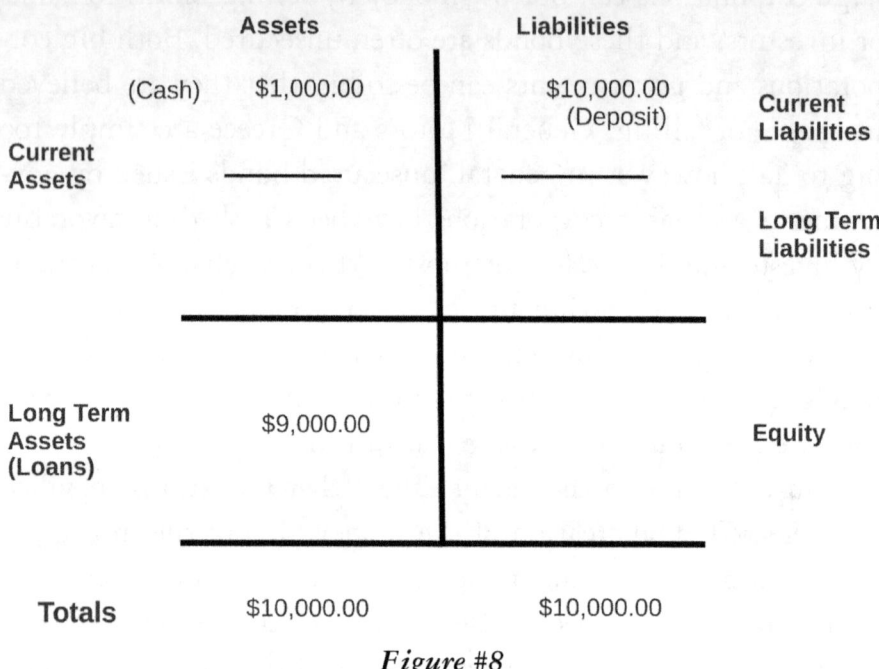

Figure #8

The balance sheet clearly shows that your bank did indeed create an additional $9,000.00 in demand deposits, which, added to your $1,000.00 in cash, now totals $10,000.00 in deposits. At the same time, we have created $9,000.00 in loans, which have ended up in the demand deposits. It really doesn't matter where the money is deposited; the multiplier effect of money still happens, and the balance sheet for the above scenario looks exactly like the composite balance for all the banks we looked at in the last chapter.

Now suppose that when you deposited your $1,000.00 in cash at the bank, the bank determined that having $1,000.00

in cash in its vault meant that this amount was now its reserve requirement and made a $9,000.00 loan, which was deposited back into one of its accounts. If you put this scenario on a balance sheet, the balance sheet will appear identical to the one above, as well as to the composite bank balance sheet we looked at in the last chapter. In reality it is probably illegal for the bank to assume that the $1,000.00 in cash is their reserve. This would be truly creating money out of thin air. My point in putting it in print is to show that the results from creating money out of thin air is the same as either of the two ways that the bank or banks could legally do this. Any way you cut it would be the same which is to say that banks really do create money out of thin air, but, yes, it is backed by something which makes it created out of the not so thin air.

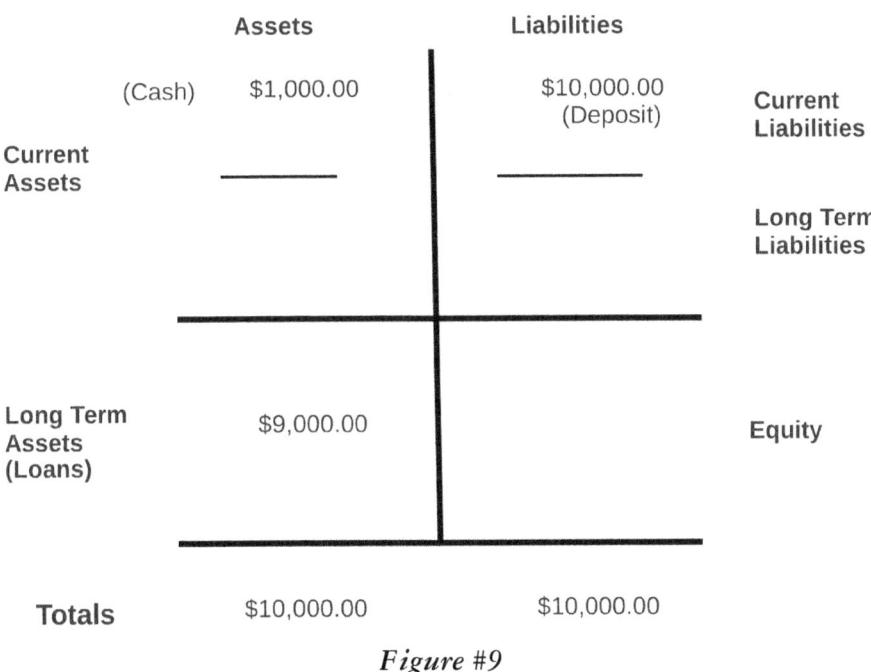

Figure #9

This is in reality the way the multiplier effect happens. It doesn't really matter whether your bank loans out $900.00 of your cash that you deposited, considering $100.00 as its reserve requirement and the deposits are made in a series of banks or one after the other at the same bank—it all comes out the same in the end. However, in the second example, your bank has cut all the other banks out of the picture. Whichever method you use doesn't matter; the money is created and backed by loans, which makes it not quite so thin air.

I have presented two different scenarios concerning the multiplier effect. First your bank loans out $900.00 of your deposit. In this scenario the money to cover the loan comes out of your deposit account. The asset behind the loan has been paid for and is no longer the bank's concern. What is the bank's concern is how to deal with the fact that you only have $100.00 left in your account when there is really supposed to be $1,000.00.

In the first scenario, the second bank receives $900.00 of the cash you originally deposited in your account, and it now loans out 90% ($816.00) of the deposited cash to someone else. The process continues on down the line through the succession of loans, each bank having paid for the asset behind its loan in cash. All these banks have to do is cover the 90% of the deposit that is loaned out and forget about the asset purchased. The asset is paid for and will produce an income stream the bank can now use. The composite balance sheet shows the creation of the extra $9,000.00 in demand deposits, which the combined banks will have to cover, but all the assets are paid for and the banks don't have to pay attention to covering the cost of the asset.

In the second scenario, the bank uses all $1,000.00 as its cash reserve by making a series of loans that are deposited back into accounts at the bank and creates $9,000.00 in loans and deposits. Since the asset or assets behind the loans is paid for with money that came out of thin air, in reality the payment was probably made in the form of a check, the asset is also paid for, and the bank doesn't have to worry about the financing of the asset or money tied up in it. The only thing the bank now has to worry about is covering the added $9,000.00 in new deposits of money that is only on the books. The last sentence is technically correct. The bank will technically deposit $9,000.00 into the account of the individual or business borrowing the money and at the same time the $9,000.00 will be spent on the asset or assets leaving the depositors account with $9,000.00 less and the bank will have to cover this money that essentially came out of the depositors account.

In either of the these scenarios, the assets behind the loans are paid for and are not a big concern for the bank unless they start losing value. All the bank needs to worry about is coming up with money to pay for the purchases that all the depositors are making with the money in their demand accounts and the $1,000.00 reserve requirement it must maintain.

There is one other point that I ought to make at this point. In Describing the multiplier effect of money I have used two points of view: one is what happens with your single deposit at your bank and the other is what happens as a composite in a number of banks. Your bank will receive other deposits besides yours and some of these deposits will be the second third or fourth loans in a series of loans started at other banks. Your bank's balance sheet, as well as every other bank's balance sheet, will in the end, look like the composite balance sheet we have looked at. In a perfectly random world each bank would receive its relative portion, based on the size of its total deposits, of all the money created out of thin air. Banks don't function in a perfectly random world but each bank has thousands of deposits and money coming and going and the balance sheet of each will be more like the composit balance sheet than the one we produced for your deposit at your bank.

Economists use the definition of the multiplier effect of money to explain two things: the first is how banks create money and how much they will create, which has been explained; the second is to explain how a central bank can increase of decrease the amount of money in the economy. Increasing or decreasing the amount of money and why they so is the subject of later chapter.

At this point you are probably seeing all kinds of red flags and saying, yes, but you are forgetting something. No, I haven't forgotten anything; I just haven't gotten to it yet. There are in reality many different things going on here that all need to be understood simultaneously. Unfortunately I can't give it to you all at one time; it is simply beyond my abilities. I would ask you to persevere and continue to the next chapter. Eventually we will cover everything, and things will make a lot more sense then, if they don't now. Until then, hang in there.

Juggling takes great concentration.
Nothing ruins your act quite like dropping the balls!

THE GREAT JUGGLING ACT

You do not have to be terribly astute, once you understand the multiplier effect of money, to figure out that the last scenario from the previous chapter left the bank with your $1,000.00 dollars in cash from your demand deposit and $9,000.00 worth of additional demand deposits as well. The $9,000.00 in deposits is only on the books; there is no currency backing it, yet, because every depositor can claim and use the $10,000.00 in their accounts, they are going to spend their money left and right, just as fast as they can, because it is their money, and the money is available to take out of the bank. Yet the bank has already paid out most of the money from all these demand deposits to create the loans and or pay for the assets. So how can the bank pay for the goods, services or assets the depositors have purchased if the money only exists on paper?

There are three things happening simultaneously here, so first let's look at the loans. Loans are financial instruments. They have legal rights associated with them and also income streams. A mortgage on a house produces a payment every month that goes to the bank that holds the mortgage. The loan and mortgage can be viewed as an income stream of so much money every month for the duration of the loan. Because the loan has value, an income stream, and legal status (the property legally belongs to the holder of the mortgage until the loan is paid off), the loan (income stream) together with the mortgage can be bought and sold. The income from loans (deposits) within a well-established bank is probably a daily occurrence, which helps the bank to pay for the goods and services the depositors are buying.

Second, we need to look at the bank. The bank has money coming in from the loans it has made. There are also retailers that make deposits every day. You and all the other depositors are also adding your paychecks or money to your bank accounts at varying intervals. This presents a picture of money coming and going in all directions at the same time, and keeping track of all this money is no easy task—welcome to the world of banking. The important idea is that the bank always has money coming in as well as going out.

The third thing that bears on a bank's ability to pay for the depositors' purchases is equity. In the beginning, when a bank is first established, the Federal Reserve requires that the owners of the bank put up huge sums of cash, called equity. The equity is in reality a reserve so the bank can pay for all the things the depositors are spending their money on. Once the bank gets to a certain size, it has so many loans and deposits and fees all coming and going that it can rob Peter to pay Paul today and tomorrow rob Paul to repay Peter. The process of shuffling the money around creates what I choose to call float. Float is simply the breathing room created between when you have to pay for something and when you actually get the money to pay for it. Banks depend on float; it is one of the ways in which they make money. At the end of the day, the only things that matter to the bank are that the bills were paid by the money coming in and that the bank has enough money to cover its reserve requirement. It doesn't matter whose money your bank has or doesn't have; it only has to meet the two criteria of paying everything as it comes in and having enough money to cover the reserve requirement. Of all the money in the deposits, 90% is only on paper, so the bank doesn't have to have any of that 90% on hand. It really needs to have only the reserve requirement on hand in cash. The process is one great big juggling act. It gets to be so big in fact that no one can really keep track of what is happening as it is happening. Try juggling 3 balls at one time, and then try juggling 250. How does the bank do it? It has a savior: the Federal Reserve.

So how does the Federal Reserve help them keep track of what is going on with their money? If you remember, way back in the second chapter, I explained that the Federal Reserve is a central bank and one of its functions is that of a clearing house for all money moving between banks. Big Brother—in this case the Federal Reserve—really does know *where* the banks' money is coming from and going to and *when* it is coming or going. The Federal Reserve doesn't really care why or for what purpose all the money is moving around, but it knows where every penny of it is at any given point in time. And of course it knows what share of it belongs to your bank as well as to every other bank.

Please remember that you deposited $1,000.00 in cash in your bank, and the bank still has all of that cash in its vaults as its reserve requirement. All the money moving around out there is the nonexistent money that was created out of thin air, which in reality exists only on the books. I say "nonexistent," but it really is money, it really is being spent, and individuals really are taking home the goods they buy with this nonexistent money. It is nonexistent because it is not currency; it is only on the books.

The Federal Reserve District Bank that oversees your bank tells your bank twice a day, once in the morning and once in the afternoon, where it stands on its reserve requirements. There are 12 districts, each represented by a District Federal Reserve Bank, in the Federal Reserve and your bank is supervised by one of them. Remember that all the money coming and going is the nonexistent money. The cash reserve required doesn't actually go anywhere. It stays in the vault at your bank. Your reserve requirement is like a credit card limit. The Federal Reserve Bank will overdraft your bank's account at the Federal Reserve Bank by up to what your bank has in cash reserves in its vaults. If the Federal Reserve Bank has processed $2,000.00 leaving your bank, and your bank only has $1500.00 coming in, it will tell your bank that the bank now has only $500.00 in reserves ($2,000.00 − $1,500.00 = $500.00), which is figuratively subtracted from your reserve of $1,000.00, leaving the bank with only $500.00 in reserves). Understand that ten minutes from now, the balance could be reversed because of all the money changing hands so fast between the banks. The Federal Reserve Bank will let your bank's reserve requirement go up or down on its books during the course of the day without your bank being penalized, and the Federal Reserve Bank is kind enough to let every bank know twice a day where it stands, midmorning and midafternoon, so the bank has time to maneuver.

We have kind of gotten away from your bank and into the Federal Reserve, but it is important to understand every step in this process as we go along, or you will get lost. Every step is important.

At the end of every day, the Federal Reserve District Bank knows where your bank stands in relation to your bank's reserve requirement. This is an important part of the Federal Reserve regulatory responsibility. Of course if your bank has all its reserves or more on paper, at the Federal Reserve District

Bank there is no problem and the Federal Reserve District Bank politely ignores your bank until tomorrow. If your bank does not have all of its necessary reserves at the end of the day, consider two scenarios. First, your bank's remaining reserves are between $1.00 and $999.00 ($1,000.00 required) at the end of the day. If your bank's reserves fall into this category, your bank is breaking the law. It is a law that every bank has to maintain one-tenth of all its demand deposits in its vaults or on deposit in the Federal Reserve vaults. In this case an officer at your bank will receive a telephone call from someone at the Federal Reserve District Bank as a friendly reminder that your bank is currently breaking the law. The Federal Reserve District Bank will also send a letter to another of the bank's officers to let him or her know of the infraction. If your bank happens to end the day with less than its reserve requirement two days in a row, the bank will get two letters and two calls from different individuals at the Federal Reserve District Bank. If it happens three days in a row, the following day the bank will find a Federal Reserve Bank auditor waiting at the door first thing in the morning. The auditor is trained and competent and will know, probably within half an hour, whether he or she should exercise his or her authority and close the doors of the bank. It is serious business. In reality I believe a bank can only be under its reserve requirement three times in any ten-day period before the auditor shows up. For the purposes of understanding what is happening at the bank, the principle is more important than the time interval.

In the second scenario, consider what happens if your bank's reserve is negative at the end of the day. Not only is your bank breaking the law, but your bank also no longer has any cash reserves on the Federal Reserve District Bank's books and has exceeded its credit limit with the Federal Reserve and with no cash, your bank is belly-up, insolvent, and bankrupt. The juggler has dropped the balls, and the act is up! The reserve requirement is not only important; it is serious, to the point of being everything. The great juggling act is real, and if at the end of the day the bank's reserve requirement disappears on the books at the Federal Reserve District Bank, the bank really is history, even though the bank still has $1,000.00 in cash in its vaults. The $1,000.00 in the bank's vaults in reality now belongs to the Federal Reserve Bank, and your bank still owes anything the $1,000.00 didn't cover.

Originally we were on the subject of how the bank is able to keep track of all the money coming and going. Your bank's Federal Reserve District Bank keeps track of it for them, and I hope it is clear how it keeps track of it. The bank still has to keep track of all the money on its books, which is its primary accounting responsibility, but the Federal Reserve Bank keeps track of its reserve requirements in relation to all the money that is coming and going. It does the same for every other bank and lets them know twice a day where they stand. By knowing where it stands the bank also has a good idea of what it will need to do to keep the Federal Reserve District Bank off its back at the end of the day, which is what the next chapter is all about.

This could be the end of the chapter on the great juggling act, but there is one more piece of information that you might enjoy knowing. Money has velocity. Velocity is the speed with which money turns over, or the speed with which it returns to its theoretical beginning place. It is questionable whether money ever returns to its original starting place, but that is the theoretical idea. Suppose for a minute that the velocity of money were to double. This would mean that the amount of money being spent in that time period would also double. There would also be twice as much money moving between banks through the Federal Reserve. As far as the great juggling act goes, it is still a simple case of robbing Peter to pay Paul and then turning around and robbing Paul to pay Peter—only this time you do it twice every day instead of just once. Think of it as your $1,000.00 cash that you received in pay. You will spend it all over the course of a month and then receive another $1,000.00 from your employer to replace it, and you start all over again. The turnaround time to regain your money, probably not the same bills, was thirty days plus or minus. Money is constantly changing hands. If it were to suddenly change hands twice as fast, its velocity would double. By doubling the velocity of money, you technically double the amount of money that is created out of thin air. All the money moving between banks is now moving twice as many times, increasing and depleting demand deposits twice as fast. On paper the total economy has now spent twice the amount of money as before.

This means that instead of $9,000.00 in demand deposits on the books, there is now $18,000.00 on the books. When or if the velocity doubled, it would require that there be another $1,000.00 in cash in the banks' vault or in its account at the Federal Reserve to meet the reserve requirement on the $18,000.00 moving around in the economy. The Federal Reserve Bank has ways of injecting cash into the economy or banks so that the extra cash needed to compensate for the extra money created by velocity is covered, but I will say more about that in later chapters. In other words, velocity also has an effect on the multiplier effect. How economists calculate or guess the rate of velocity is beyond the scope of this book, so I won't even go there. There is, however, no such thing as negative velocity. It can be zero or above but not negative. Once the money has been created, it is there, and as long as the money exists on the books, its velocity will be zero or more.

I mention velocity here because the greater the velocity, the greater the speed at which the juggler must juggle, the greater the potential for float, the greater the potential for profit on the part of the bank, and the faster the great juggling act can come to an abrupt end.

You and I as individuals are not allowed to create money or use float like banks do. Therefore why would you ever believe it was legal for a bank to do it, much less possible for the bank to achieve? The truth is that banks do it every day, and until you accepts the concept as real, you will never understand what banks do and why it is not only important to all of us but also why it can and does on occasion get out of hand and cause serious problems. Believe that the great juggling act is real!

In any endeavor that invites serious risk,
it is not only comforting but prudent to have a safety net.

OVERNIGHT LOANS

In the juggling act that I have described, it is simply a matter of luck as to how much money goes out and how much money comes in every day. Your bank is simply gambling, playing the law of averages. If you work with the law of averages, sooner or later you will lose, for losing, at least some of the time, is written into the game when you play the law of averages. Bankers understood they were playing with fire, so they did the logical thing and found a way to borrow money to cover themselves when the law of averages catches up to them.

In the banking business, your bank will develop a network of banks it can call on for financial help, and those banks in turn will call on your bank when they need money. The loans between these banks are called overnight loans. Your bank borrows the money today, and tomorrow your bank pays it back. It is a very simple loan, and between banks these loans are unsecured. There is no collateral backing up an overnight loan. There is no red tape; no long, messy trail of paperwork; no hassle; and it is almost instantaneous (a slight exaggeration). The idea is that it is a quick, easy loan that can be made on the spur of the moment anytime, to tide you over till the next morning so that the Federal Reserve District Bank (and everyone else) won't know your bank is running low on money. Someone at your bank gets on the phone and asks his counterpart at the other bank for a loan, and it is a done deal. With a network of banks, if Bank X doesn't have the money to loan, then Bank Y or Z probably will. If there ever comes a time when your bank doesn't pay back its overnight loan the next morning, word gets around very quickly. In the banking industry, you don't miss paying off an overnight loan—ever! Every bank uses overnight loans, and everyone scratches everyone else's backs, as long as they are and remain in good standing by paying back the loans the next morning.

In the end the only thing the Federal Reserve cares about is the reserve balance—whether your bank is over or under on the reserve balance. This is particularly true at the end of the day. The only thing your bank therefore needs to concern itself with is making sure it has enough money to cover its reserves. The bills need to be paid, too, but the bank's money coming in and going out is taken care of first, and the reserves are left to go up or down in accordance. So if the bank covers its reserve requirement, all is taken care of. Remember that the Federal Reserve District Bank tells your bank twice a day where it stands in relation to its reserves. The only test that is all or nothing at the end of the day happens when the Federal Reserve District Bank closes its books. Of course prudent banks always cover their bases and borrow enough to make sure their reserve requirements are met.

Let us go back to the balance sheet in Figure 5, which includes equity and is now Figure 10 on page 38.

In Figure 10 the only thing the bank has to cover is the $1,000.00 in cash on the left side of the balance sheet. Let's suppose that the bank estimates that with all the money coming and going, it will only have $700.00 left in reserves at the end of the day. With only $700.00 in cash, the new balance sheet would look like the one in Figure 11. You will notice that the bank has

	Assets		Liabilities	
(Cash)	$1,000.00		$10,000.00 (Deposit)	Current Liabilities
Current Assets	———		———	
(Stock)	$1,000.00			Long Term Liabilities
Long Term Assets (Loans)	$9,000.00		$1,000.00	Equity
Totals	$11,000.00		$11,000.00	

Figure #10

	Assets		Liabilities	
(Cash)	$700.00		$10,000.00 (Deposit)	Current Liabilities
Current Assets	———		———	
(Stock)	$1,000.00			Long Term Liabilities
Long Term Assets (Loans)	$9,000.00		$700.00	Equity
Totals	$10,700.00		$10,700.00	

Figure #11

actually lost $300.00 on the left side of its balance sheet. In order to get the balance sheet to balance, $300.00 must also be removed from the right side of the balance sheet. Since you still have 1,000.00 deposited in your account, the only thing that can change is equity. Whenever the bank loses money or comes up short of money on the left-hand side of the balance sheet, the loss always comes out of equity on the right-hand side of the balance sheet. This leaves the balance at the bottom of the balance sheet showing $10,700.00. The fact that losses always come out of equity is an important concept to remember. In order to insure it had $1,000.00 in reserves at the end of the day your bank would decide to borrow $350.00 in the form of an overnight loan to cover its reserve requirement. After borrowing the $350.00, the balance sheet would now look like the one in Figure 12.

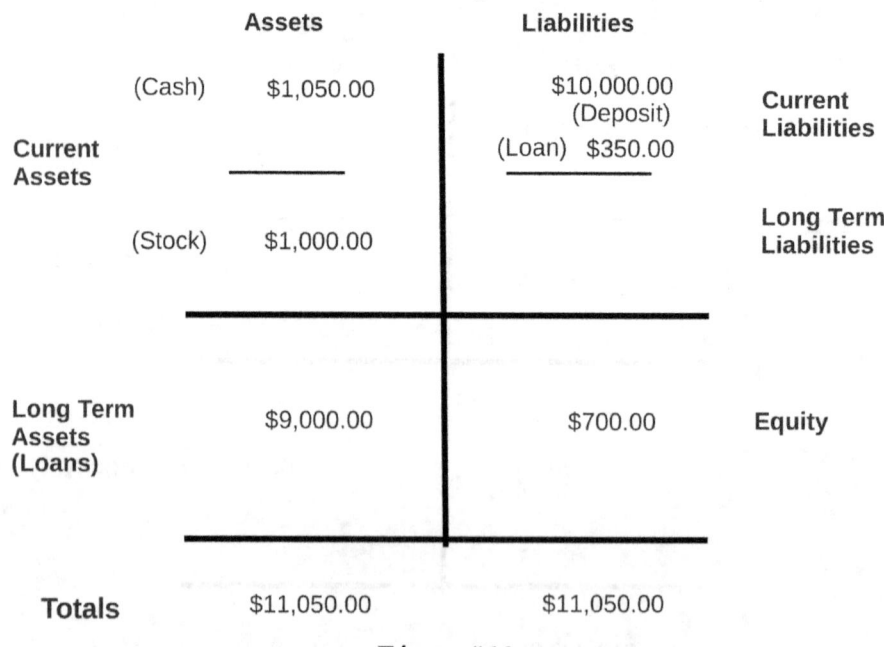

	Assets	Liabilities	
(Cash)	$1,050.00	$10,000.00 (Deposit)	Current Liabilities
Current Assets	————	(Loan) $350.00 ————	
(Stock)	$1,000.00		Long Term Liabilities
Long Term Assets (Loans)	$9,000.00	$700.00	Equity
Totals	$11,050.00	$11,050.00	

Figure #12

The bank has borrowed $350.00, and it is a loan, so it goes on the right-hand side of the balance sheet. Since it is an overnight loan and will be repaid the next day, it is a short-term loan. The $350.00 in cash from the loan goes on the left-hand side and is added to the $700.00 in cash reserves that your bank still has. The bank now has more than the $1,000.00 necessary cash reserves and the balance at the bottom of the sheet is now $11,050.00 on both sides. The next morning money will start moving again, and it will be coming and going like crazy. In the process your bank will repay the loan, and the process will start all over again.

The important idea behind the overnight loan is to get just enough to get you by. At times a bank may need to borrow the complete amount of its demand deposits because all the account holders had the Girl Scout cookies they ordered last month delivered on the same day and spent everything in their accounts. At other times the stars will shine on the bank and the planets all line up, and it won't have to borrow any money at all. The bottom line is all it has to do is cover the reserves and float the rest.

If your bank takes out an overnight loan from Bank X, the Federal Reserve will see the money pass from Bank X to your bank but will have no idea why it passed between the two. The Federal Reserve Bank doesn't really know or care how your bank is run as long as it meets its reserve requirement and of course pays its bills. (There are other requirements your bank also must meet, but we will save them for later.)

When it comes to overnight loans, the Federal Reserve is the bank of last resort. A bank can always go to its Federal Reserve District Bank to get an overnight loan if necessary. The Federal Reserve sets its own interest rate on overnight loans that it makes to banks and publishes that rate. The Federal Reserve interest rate then becomes the base rate from which all banks decide how much they will charge for their overnight loans. Banks don't like to pay interest, so they try to avoid overnight loans if they can, but to be on the safe side it is better to take out a loan than come up short at the end of the day and have to deal with the Federal Reserve District Bank.

No banker wants to take out an overnight loan with the Federal Reserve District Bank simply because the Federal Reserve Bank will then know or can at least guess at the bank's financial condition. No one wants to alarm Big Brother in the regulatory world of banking. It is bad karma.

The overnight loan is the safety net that allows the great juggling act to go on indefinitely. Without the overnight loans, the juggling act would be up, and the bank would be out of business. It might be of interest to you to know there is a big word in banking jargon for running out of money to keep the juggling act afloat—"liquidity"—and it is usually used with another word, either "crisis" or "problem." Now I hope you will have an idea of the meaning when you hear or see the phrase "liquidity crisis" or "liquidity problem" used by the media in reference to banks.

One can ask the question, why doesn't an overnight loan have to cover all the money in the bank's demand deposits? First of all, in the example of your $1,000.00 deposit, your account balance will not go to *zero* the next day. In fact it probably won't go to *zero* at any time during the next thirty days. If halfway through the month you still have 25% of your money in the bank, on the books, the bank doesn't have to cover that 25% because you haven't spent it yet. The bank may have already spent it, but you haven't.

Another reason is float. If the Federal Reserve is open for only eight hours a day, money is only moving between banks for eight hours, and if the Federal Reserve is closed on Saturdays and Sundays, your bank can float money all weekend long. Your bank can be open as long as it wishes, and you, the consumer, can spend your money all day, every day, but the money will only change hands while its Federal Reserve District Bank is open. The rest of the time the bank can float the money. While the Federal Reserve District Bank is open, your bank must be on its toes and make sure it has its reserve requirement at the end of the Federal Reserve District Bank's day.

Another interesting occurrence, using an extreme example, is what happens to the reserve requirement if the bank's demand deposits were to go to zero. I posed this question earlier when I mentioned all the demand deposit holders using all their deposits to buy Girl Scout cookies on the same day. When I cited this example earlier, we were looking at the outflow of money from the bank and how the bank might have to cover the outflow through its overnight loans. This time, however, we are looking at the reserve requirement. If demand deposits were to go to zero, the reserve requirement would also go to zero. This would leave the bank in the position where it needed no cash in its vault to cover its reserve requirement. This is an extreme example, but the corollary is that if demand deposits decrease, reserve requirements also decrease, as does the amount of money needed in overnight loans to cover the reserve requirement. Of course if demand deposits have all been spent, the bank will be suddenly covering lots of newly written checks and debit card entries and may need to borrow overnight to cover the outflow of money. As reserve requirements decrease, overnight loans shift from covering reserves to covering actual spending by account holders.

After mentioning the extreme idea of a banks demand deposits going to zero, it might be nice to know the Federal Reserve District Bank sets the reserve requirement for a bank every ten to fourteen days. During that interval the Federal Reserve District Bank does not lower or raise the reserve requirement. To change the reserve requirement on an instantaneous or real time basis as transactions happened would create a situation of *EXTREME* financial volatility, not to mention the need for extreme computational capabilities just to keep track of the changes.

Float also works when you consider where you spend your money. If you write a check at the grocery store, the money isn't really spent until the check makes it to the Federal Reserve District Bank and your money is actually transferred back through the Federal Reserve District Bank. If the check is in limbo for twenty-four hours, it creates twenty-four hours of float. If you buy everything on your credit card and make only one payment a month, paying off the entire balance of your credit card, all that unspent money theoretically, sits in your bank account, most likely for a day or even much longer. Float happens, and the bank takes all it can get. If you spend money in New York and live in San Francisco, the money will have to go through two district banks, which may even slow the transfer down further.

My bank also has a policy for large transfers of money. If I deposit a check for more than $3,000.00 in the bank, it makes me wait for up to five days before the entire amount is credited to my account. The bank does this in part to make sure the money really does get transferred. Meanwhile my money is in limbo, and so is the money of the person who wrote me the check. This is float, and as long as the money is in limbo, the bank doesn't have to cover it with an overnight loan. In the same vein, when I deposit a check after two o'clock in the afternoon at my bank, the money is not credited to my account until the next day, even if the check does make it through the Federal Reserve District Bank that day. This can also create float.

On average in the real world a bank may only be able to float 50% to 90% of its demand deposits, and every bank could be different. Back in the second chapter, my friend Michael believed the bank borrowed the money and then loaned it out and the bank's profit was the difference between the two interest rates. If the overnight loans amounted to 100% of deposits every night, this scenario, as presented by Michael, would be true in reverse. Instead of borrowing the money first, as in Michael's story, the bank is making the loan first and then borrowing the money. But once again this would be merely shuffling money around, not multiplying it, and from the bank's standpoint, the bank wants to maximize profits, and the incentive is to float 90% of demand deposits 100% of the time.

The bank has multiplied money ten times and is making interest on all the loans it has made without having to cover (borrow money) to do so most of the time.

The questioning mind always asks why!
And oh, how glorious and painful is the answer!
Glorious because of the light and knowledge that it brings,
painful because the answer yields only more questions!
—Anonymous

WHY?

Why? Why do banks do all this? It is risky, not to mention a lot of work. Seriously, if you can't see the seriousness of the risks your bank takes as well as the fact that it takes a lot of effort to make it all work, you really don't understand what is going on. As for why they do all this, first, every individual or entity that exists must justify its existence. If no one thinks you should exist, in all probability you won't exist for very long. This is especially true with businesses. If you are ignored by your customers, you will eventually cease to exist. Banks justify their existence by providing services to you and me. That is the bottom line. If you didn't want to own a home, buy a car, or have a place to deposit your money and earn interest, there would be no need for a bank. Banks, relatively speaking, are safe places to keep your money until you spend it. It is also more convenient to carry a debit card or a checkbook than to carry a wad of cash. Face it—the banks provide us with services that we want and ultimately feel we need. Second, there is money for the banks in doing it, as long as they are careful and prudent. Everyone works for gain, whether it is payment for labor or profit from doing business. Banks are in it for the profit, just like you and me.

Of course that begs the question of how they make money. My friends in the second chapter seemed to think that banks made their money from interest, and they certainly do make some of their money from interest, as well as fees. In recent years interest rates have been so low that you might even ask why the banks would make loans at all. The fact is interest isn't what they are really after. What most people don't see is the real prize at the end of the rainbow. If you understand the multiplier effect of money, the real prize lies in the loans (the value of the assets) the banks create. The loan value of the asset is called principal. They are after the principal. Think about it. They use your demand deposits to create a loan, which in turn creates an income stream. Who owns that income stream or the collateral behind it? The bank does! It will eventually receive in return not only the interest but also the principal amount of the loan. The bank loans out $9,000.00 because you deposit $1,000.00 in the bank, which is now its reserve. This will create $9,000.00 in money on the bank's books. Since the bank owns the financial instrument (loan) and the income stream from the loan or the collateral behind the loan in case of default, it will eventually make $9,000.00 plus interest and any fees associated with the loan as the loan is paid off. The bank has not only created wealth out of thin air, but the bank owns—either as collateral until the loan is paid off or in cash that it will have received as principal and interest payments—the financial instrument that it created. So why does the bank do all this? Because it creates wealth for the bank and its owners!

The bank, in creating a loan, is not really after the interest. It is after the principal. While it does make a gain, income, from interest, it doesn't really matter what the interest rate is; if the interest rate were 1% it would still make the principal. Banks will make loans no matter how low the interest rate goes simply because they are after the principal, not the interest.

I should note here that interest is established by supply, demand, and risk. Supply and demand move interest rates up and down, not necessarily the banks.

We should also look at a loan and how it is paid off. Suppose you bought a home for $100,000.00 to be paid back over thirty years, you didn't have to make a down payment, and you pay on average $1,000.00 in interest every year. I am being unrealistic in the way I'm simplifying the process, but just follow along. The bank would pay whomever you were buying the house from the $100,000.00 you borrowed. Of that amount 100% would be hot air. The bank must keep 10% of demand deposits in its vault, but the loan amount is all hot air. In one sense we can say that the bank's interest in the loan is 10%—the amount of the bank's capital (money) that is tied up and can't be used because it a part of the reserve. In other words this is the bank's actual investment in the loan. Over the course of the loan, the bank will earn the principal and interest on the loan. In the example I gave, the bank will make $130.000.00 over the course of the loan ($30,000.00 in interest, $1,000.00 per year for thirty years + $100,000.00 in principal). The bank's annual rate of return on its investment of $10,000.00 (the reserve amount) is $130,000 divided by 30 or $4,333.33/year. That is 43% of the bank's actual investment before expenses each year. That is not a bad annual rate of return on the bank's investment.

Now let's take a look at another possible scenario. Take the same situation as above, but after ten years you get another job in a far-off place and sell your home and pay off the loan. You will have paid $100,000.00 in principal plus $10,000.00 in interest for a total of $110,000.00. The annual rate of return on investment for the bank would now be $110,000 divided by ten years or $11,000.00 per year. That amounts to a 110% average return on the bank's investment every year. Much better, no?

What would happen if the bank turned around and sold the loan the very next day after you took it out? The loan would likely be sold to an insurance company or another investor that is interested in the interest on the loan. What the insurance company really wants is the income stream. The insurance company will not pay the full amount, so let's say the bank sells the loan to the insurance company for $90,000.00 instead of the face amount of $100,000.00. This would be referred to as the mortgage being sold at a 10% or a $10,000.00 discount; a discount is about getting something for less than it is worth. Since the insurance company is really buying an income stream, it will get payments on a $100,000.00 loan for which it only paid $90,000.00. The net effect for the insurance company is that the interest it receives on the $90,000.00 it paid will go up significantly. For example, if the monthly payment on the $100,000.00 loan were $500.00, and the monthly payment on a $90,000.00 loan were $450.00, the insurance company would be making an extra $50.00 per month on its $90,000.00 loan. As far as the insurance company is concerned, this $50.00 extra per month is in reality extra interest. If the original interest rate on the $100,000.00 loan were 4%, then the new interest rate would be somewhere near 8% or double the 4% rate. In this day and age, if the interest the insurance company is making goes up to 8%, it is making good money. Please note that the insurance company paid cash for the purchase of the loan;

it was not another loan. In this example the bank would only make $90,000.00; after one day and there is no interest paid to the bank. The bank's annual rate of return on its investment would be $90,000.00 divided by 1/365th of a year (the one day it held the loan). I'll let you do the math on that one, but trust me when I say the rate of return is huge. If you have purchased a home in the last twenty years, the loan was probably sold to some investment or insurance company within one year of the time you bought it. Do you now understand why the bank would sell the loan? The faster the bank can turn over a loan, the greater the profit for the bank. It changes that nonexistent money, which is tied up in the principal of the loan, into cash, and the sooner it's done, the sooner it has actually earned it.

At this point let's stop and look at your bank's balance sheet. Because the bank will be taking a loss, we will use the balance sheet we created in the chapter on the multiplier effect of money (Figure #5), which has $1,000.00 in equity. The balance sheet contains a loan for $9,000.00. Let's assume a customer had bought a house—OK, for $9,000.00 it would only be a very nice dollhouse—and the next day, the bank sells the loan to an insurance company for $8,000.00. The balance sheet in Figure #13 will show the results after the sale.

The bank now has lost $1,000.00 in assets. It also has $8,000.00 in cash from the sale, which it adds to the $1,000.00 it already had, for a total of $9,000.00 in the form of cash. To make the new balance sheet balance, the right side of the balance sheet must lose $1,000.00. Of course deposits have not changed, so the money must come from equity. The $1,000.00 will come out of equity, which leaves the bank's equity at zero. This is called deleveraging. Deleveraging and equity are subjects of the next two chapters, and I will leave the discussion of these two items until then. What is important about this

	Assets		Liabilities	
	Assets		**Liabilities**	
	(Cash)	$9,000.00	$10,000.00 (Deposit)	Current Liabilities
Current Assets		——	——	
	(Stock)	$1,000.00		Long Term Liabilities
Long Term Assets (Loans)			$ 00.00	Equity
Totals		$10,000.00	$10,000.00	

Figure #13

transaction is that the bank, with $8,000.00 in cash, can now claim the cash as reserves and make loans of $81,000.00 in the near term. By selling the $9,000.00 loan for $8,000.00, it can exchange that $1,000.00 loss for another $72,000.00 in loans and the income stream associated with it. That is a good rate of exchange if you can absorb the initial $1,000.00 loss.

At this point I probably ought to make a remark or two about the interest that banks charge. There are a number of ways in which banks structure interest payments. Most home loans have some form of amortized payments, which means that the interest is figured monthly on the remaining balance of the loan. A fixed payment every month means that at the beginning about 99% of your monthly payment is an interest payment, and 1% of your payment goes to pay off the balance of the loan. The bottom line is that you pay the majority of the interest on the loan in the first ten years of your loan while paying nearly nothing of the principal of your loan. This is a good deal for the bank if you sell your home within the first ten years because you still owe at least 90% of your loan's principal and have already paid a huge amount of the total interest. I previously stated that banks aren't after the interest, but by using an amortized basis for the interest payment, they get a lot more of it in the first years of the loan, which sweetens the deal for the bank. I learned in one of my finance classes in college that the average age of a home loan when it was sold was seven years, that was in the 1970's. In a mobile society, people are selling their homes on a frequent basis so they can move up the ladder or somewhere where the climate is nicer or the grass is greener.

Banks are in the business of making money in more ways than one. They certainly do make money from interest and fees and have over the years developed ways to make as much as possible from both of them. But the real interest they have in banking is defined by the multiplier effect of money, which allows them to create money and the financial assets that back that money. Eventually the person or persons who wish to hold those assets will repay the bank for having created them.

Once again you should be thinking that I just messed up on my thinking. It should be obvious that the money paid out to obtain the loans (read assets) was put into demand deposits somewhere, and in this case, to simplify, let's assume the money was all deposited back into your bank. Again, as an example, we will use your bank with your $1,000.00 deposit. You made the deposit, the bank used your money as its reserve, and a loan was made for $9,000.00 and deposited back into your bank. That leaves us with $10,000.00 in demand deposits that have to be paid back— eventually– because that money is all tied up in the asset (loan) at the moment. In other words the money a bank collects on the income stream from the loans must go to pay off the demand deposits, which leaves the bank owning nothing but the interest. So much for the bank owning the asset, right? Wrong!

Two things happen simultaneously. But first you must understand that the bank's objective is not to pay back the demand deposit. The object is to pay for whatever the owner of the demand deposit is purchasing, which is completely different in nature than paying back the depositor. Of the two things that happen simultaneously, one is short-term and the other is longer-term in nature, but both are ongoing and generally self-perpetuating. The first is the overnight loan. It is short-term and covers the bank day-by-day on an ongoing basis. The second is that demand deposits are self-renewing over the longer term. If you deposit your $1,000.00 paycheck in the bank every month, the loan (your deposit is a loan) is renewed every month and never has to be paid off. As long as the money borrowed from demand deposits is renewed on a regular basis, the income stream from the asset never has to be used to pay off the depositor. The bank may have to pay for purchases you have made from the money you have deposited every month, but the bank has the overnight loans to get the bank over the rough spots, and if you deposit your check at the beginning of the next month, the loan is once more renewed. So the bank never has to pay off the loan (deposit) and in effect really does own the asset. The idea that the bank never has to repay the depositor sounds crazy, but that is exactly what the multiplier effect is all about. The bank views the deposit as a loan, and if you renew the loan every month, all the bank has to do is keep the great juggling act going, shuffling the money around between the deposits.

Confused? I don't blame you, so let me explain this from another point of view. Let's assume that you spend all $1,000.00

the first month after you deposit your money in the bank. The bank obviously has to pay that money to whomever you wrote the checks, but if the bank can float the money, one day at a time, for thirty days, you will deposit another $1,000.00 in the bank, and the bank can, in effect, pay off your last month's purchases with the new deposit and start floating the checks you write on the new deposit. And it goes on and on and on. Can the bank really do this? Can the bank rob Peter today to pay Paul today and tomorrow rob Paul to repay Peter, for a month? All the bank has to do is survive one day at a time. If the bank can survive until the end of the day, it takes out an overnight loan to cover what is necessary, and it is free until the next day. But it never has to pay back the $1,000.00 in your account. Please don't forget that the bank has money coming and going in all directions, and in the ensuing float, it should be able to float your $1,000.00 deposit over the thirty days. If this doesn't sound bizarre to you, you are not normal. The risks are huge! And where the risks are huge, there are generally great profits to be made, and that is exactly why the bankers are in it. This is what the multiplier effect of money is all about.

Again, this an extreme scenario, in reality the bank may only be able to float, on average, 50% of its demand deposits over the thirty days, but even then it has multiplied money five times, and regardless of reality the banks goal is to float 90% of its deposits 100% of the time.

Looking at the big picture, the only thing the bank really cares about is whether or not its total demand deposits remain the same or increase. If they start shrinking, then it has to start paying the depositors back. If the bank's deposits are increasing, its assets are increasing at nine times the rate of the increase in demand deposits, which means times are good. If the bank starts losing deposits, it has to maintain its reserve requirement and at the same time pay out the deposits that are being taken away. This causes what is known as deleveraging.

At this point, if you want to understand *deleveraging,* we probably ought to take a serious look at *leveraging*.

A lever is a great tool.
It gives its user a great advantage against overwhelming forces.
So it is in banking.
In banking leverage is also a great tool when times are good;
however, in bad times the lever is reversed, crunching the bank itself.

LEVERAGE

I imagine every reader will conjure up in his or her mind some kind of lever when the word "leverage" is mentioned. Usually levers are used to move heavy objects laterally against friction or vertically against the pull of gravity, or both. A lever could be a crowbar or a long stick or anything long enough that when applied over a fulcrum gives the user an advantage over the weight of an object. In banking the meaning is more abstract. Simply put, one uses a small amount of money to buy a large interest in an investment. In the case of your bank and the multiplier effect of money, the bank uses your $1,000.00 deposit to create $9,000.00 in loans, which is a one-to-nine leverage rate. The bank is making nine times as much in principal and interest from the income stream it has created than it would if the only thing it could loan out was the $1,000.00 you deposited. This is leverage. And it definitely works in the favor of the bank.

Leverage, as it applies to the multiplier effect and deposits, is determined by the reserve requirement. A one-tenth reserve requirement means you can leverage your deposits out ten times because you end up with the original $1,000.00 plus an additional $9,000.00 in loans as well as deposits. If the reserve requirement were 5% or one-twentieth of deposits, you could leverage deposits out twenty times. If the reserve requirement were 20% or one-fifth of deposits, you would be leveraging deposits out at five times the amount of demand deposits. In other words the smaller the reserve requirement, the greater the leverage. Within the banking industry, which includes the Federal Reserve, the 10% reserve requirement seems to be a safe amount of reserves for a bank to hold on deposits, and it also seems to be held as safe by economists and politicians who write regulation.

The greater the rate of leverage, the greater is the risk to the bank, but also the greater the potential profits. The risk usually doesn't show up unless the loans the bank has made go bad. Loans go bad for one of two reasons. The loan officers made poor choices when they evaluated the ability of the borrower to repay the loans, or hard economic times have beset the people who took out the loans.

In good economic times, if the bank has made good loans, the bank is making great money because it is leveraged in a favorable direction. If economic times turn for the worse, the lever can get turned around, and the loans start leveraging the bank in reverse at the same rate of leverage, regardless of the diligence of the loan officers. If loans start failing or profits go way down, the lever starts squeezing the bank. When leverage reverses, what begins to happen is usually referred to as deleveraging. Deleveraging usually means some loans go bad or assets have to be devalued. As you might have guessed, deleveraging is not only painful but can also be fatal. In the next chapter, we will look at equity and what happens when a bank deleverages.

Leverage in the banking world is about loaning out someone else's money as many times as the bank legally can, which in part is determined by the reserve requirement (10% in the United States). In doing this it creates ten times the financial assets, for which it will be repaid in principal and interest. From the bank's point of view, this is the positive side of leverage.

The negative side of leverage, when the lever gets turned around, crunches the bank where it hurts the most, which is equity. Another concept is important to understand. When you use a lever to move a weight, you put the lever away when you are done, and it is over. Gravity and friction are constant forces that don't change. In banking the bank uses the lever to create marketable financial instruments and in the process puts the lever in the hands of the market, over which the bank has no control when the economy turns sour. In other words the lever is never put away after it is initially used. The bank, once having created the financial instruments through the multiplier effect, is now at the mercy of the free market and economy. When times are good the profits are great, but the economy can go into recession or worse which can wreak havoc in the banking industry.

The multiplier effect as we have used it so far has been applied to demand deposits. Leverage is really the ratio of deposits to reserves. If reserves are 10% then the leverage ratio would be ten to one. In the next chapter we will talk about equity. The multiplier effect is also applied to equity as well as deposits, however, with equity there is no reserve requirement; there is a multiplier ratio and thus leverage but no reserve requirement. In other words, at this point, we will leave behind the traditional view of the multiplier effect of money we have been talking about, and look at how the multiplier effect relates to equity.

Equity is your share of the pie
and consequently the only part you have to eat.

EQUITY

Equity is what the bank owns, which usually consists of money earned as profit and money obtained from the sale of stock. The money from demand deposits or money that the bank has borrowed actually belongs to someone else, not the bank. Equity appears on the right-hand side of a balance sheet, so assets are not listed as a part of equity either.

Earlier I mentioned that to start a bank the owners have to put up a great deal of cash. It is required by the Federal Reserve so the bank can get the process of the multiplier effect and the great juggling act started. The bank usually gets the cash from issuing stock to one or more investors.

The great juggling act takes time to warm up. As the bank grows in size, both in deposits and loans, it crosses a threshold where the bank's business becomes self-sustaining and the bank starts making a profit. As the bank makes profits in cash, it ends up with cash of its own to invest along with the money from its depositors. Now, instead of having to keep a reserve, it can loan out the profits without any reserve requirements. Reserves are only required on deposits.

In the last chapter, we looked at leverage. Leverage, when it comes to demand deposits, is determined by the reserve ratio. In terms of the bank, as a whole, leverage refers to equity, as in "the banks equity is leveraged ten times." Equity and deposits are two different things, and the leverage is different on both.

Not only can the bank leverage its money from profits, but it can also leverage money from loans that it has taken out. Most banks offer certificates of deposit. A certificate of deposit (CD) is given to an individual or business that loans money to the bank for a specific amount of time. Banks usually don't refer to CDs as loans, but that is what they are. Usually the time period for which the CD lasts varies from ninety days to ten years. As the bank borrows money in the form of CDs, the bank is free to make loans on this money at any rate of leverage it desires. If you have money in a savings account or money market account, the bank is required to count your money as demand deposits, but if you let the bank use your money as a CD where the money is tied up for a period of time, it is considered a loan.

Technically banks do not have a leverage requirement on money loaned to them or on their profits, so their money from profits and loans can be loaned out at an infinitely small ratio if the bank wishes. Since there is no reserve requirement on equity it can have zero reserves which is infinity and yes there have been and are countries in this world where there are no reserve require-ments whatever on the banks, more on that later. Of course the greater the leverage, the greater the risk, and if the people running the bank are smart and prudent, they won't let the leverage get so large that it kills the bank when times get tough.

I stated that the bank can loan out its profits and money from loans it takes out at any ratio it wishes; however, the Federal Reserve does regulate how far your bank can leverage its equity in relation to total assets, which is set at 3%. The leverage ratio on equity is figured as total equity divided by total assets (total equity / total loans (assets) and cash). Three percent equates to a

1 to 33.33 ratio. The bank can loan out its profit, which is a part of equity, and its various loans (CDs) to any extent it wishes, as long as its total assets (loans plus cash on the left side of the balance sheet) to equity ratio does not exceed 33 to 1.

I was reading an article in *The Economist* comparing American banks to European banks. It stated that American banks were healthier because they had only leveraged their equity out about thirty times (the regulation in the United States is 3% or 1 to 33.33), whereas the European banks were leveraged out about eighty times, which equates to a 1.25% equity ratio. The European banks have leveraged their equity nearly three times as much as the American banks. This means the risk of Europeans banks failing should be close to three times as great as that of American banks. If a bank has leveraged its equity in the bank out at a ratio of eighty to one, this means, in layman's terms, that if one-eightieth of the bank's loans go belly-up or the bank has to write down the value of its assets by one-eightieth, or only 1.25%, the bank has no equity left. If the bank has no equity (read ownership) in its assets, the bank is completely owned by its creditors, at which point most creditors call their loans with the bank and cut their losses. Creditors include those who have deposited their money at the bank. Even if the creditors didn't call the bank's loans, the bank regulators would shut the bank's doors because no equity means the bank has exceeded the equity to asset ratio. By the way, when depositors or creditors call their loans, it is called a run on the bank.

Once you understand this, you should be able to see why a bank doesn't like to have loans go belly-up in bad times. If the bank had made a $100,000.00 loan on your home and you couldn't make the payments, supposing hard economic times, and your house had lost 25% of its value, the bank would have to sell your house for 25% less than what the loan was taken out at. This is in effect writing the value of this particular asset (loan), a house, down by $25,000.00 and also the bank's equity by the same amount (if the left side of the balance sheet, assets, goes down, the right side of the balance sheet must also go down by the same amount and the loss comes out of equity). In dollars you have thirty times as many assets as you do equity; the leverage means if you lose just 3% of your assets you have no equity left. The lever has been reversed, being applied against the equity of the bank. If the bank writes down many loans by 25%, it will soon eat up all of the bank's equity and go through its 3% equity to loan ratio. In the recent financial crisis, homes across the nation lost on average somewhere between 25% and 40%percent of their market value. As long as the homeowners make their payments, there is no problem, but when the bank has to start foreclosing on properties and writing down its assets, it has a 3% margin of error before its equity is gone—and the bank with it. In Europe the banks only have a margin of error of 1.25%, which is not very much when assets start losing their value. Of course we have been talking about the banks losing their 3% margin in total; however, in the United States the banks only need to go below the 3% ratio and the FRB can shut their doors if it wishes.

In the United States there are also regulations on financial institutions that require that assets on their balance sheets, that are at risk, be valued according to their market value and not according to the price for which they were purchased. This means that the value of the bank's assets can be written down even without foreclosing on the property, which makes the 3% margin even more critical. After the financial crisis of 2008 most banks have been under a great deal of pressure to maintain their equity to asset ratio because they have had to write down their assets as the market value of those assets has dropped. As long as the home owner is making regular payments on time the true value of the home is dependent on its income stream and not on market value. Requiring banks to value their loans at market value forces them to recognize the potential for loss even though the loans are currently performing, which isn't always fair to the bank at the moment or when the market is in crisis mode. The riskiness of assets and equity as a counterbalance are important to the bank.

At this point we may need a pair of balance sheets to illustrate what happens when a bank writes down its assets. If you write down all of your loans by 25% (an extreme example), you still have to balance your balance sheet, which means you also have to write down the right-hand side of the balance sheet by the same amount. Some of the write-down may come in a decrease in demand deposits due to the hard economic times, but most of it will come out of equity. The loans the bank has taken out will remain the same.

In this chapter we have been talking about equity, so let's add some equity to the balance sheet we have been using. I purposely left equity out of the original balance sheets we used to describe the multiplier effect, so as not to confuse anyone, until we got to an appropriate explanation of equity and leverage. Let's add $10,000.00 to the right side of the balance sheet as equity. Equity goes in the right had column and so we must add $10,000.00 to the left hand side of the balance sheet to get it to balance. We will assume the $10,000.00 is in cash and so we will add it to the $1,000.00 in cash that we already have. We now have $11,000.00 in current assets. Our balance sheet now looks like this:

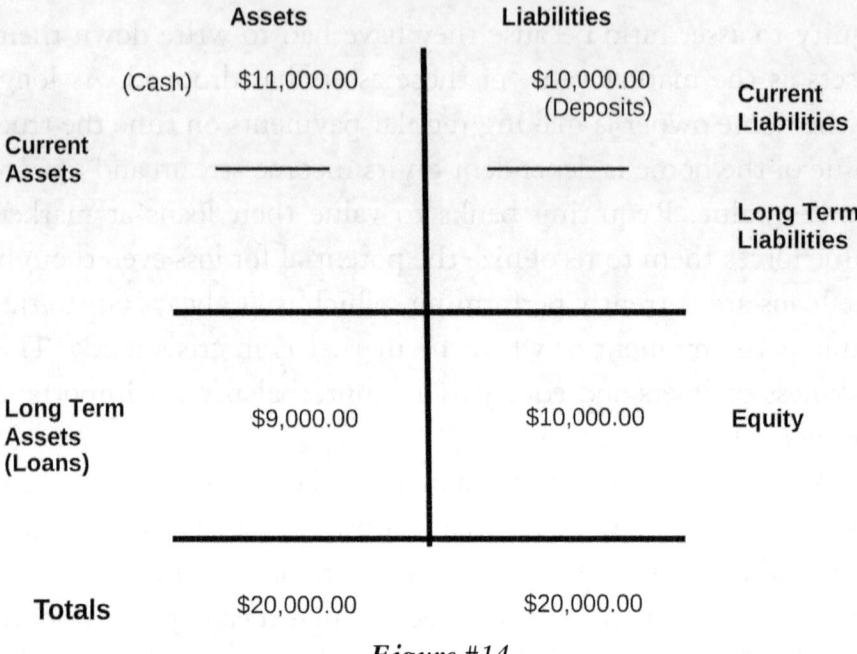

Figure #14

We have used the same balance sheet as before but added equity. Now let's go a step further and suppose that the bank issues $10,000.00 in CDs, which we discussed earlier in the chapter. CDs are loans the bank has taken out, so they go on the right side of the balance sheet. The bank now has an additional $10,000.00 in cash, which brings the total to $21,000.00 in current assets. The new balance sheet would look like figure #15.

	Assets	Liabilities	
(Cash)	$21,000.00	$10,000.00 (Deposits)	Current Liabilities
Current Assets	———	———	
		$10,000.00 (CD's)	Long Term Liabilities
Long Term Assets (Loans)	$9,000.00	$10,000.00	Equity
Totals	$30,000.00	$30,000.00	

Figure #15

At this point the bank can loan the cash from the CDs and equity in total without any reserve if it wants, as long as the equity is at least 3% of total assets. Assume that the bank loans the $20,000.00 from the CDs and equity out and the bank requires that the loans be deposited in an account at the bank. The balance sheet would now look like Figure # 16:

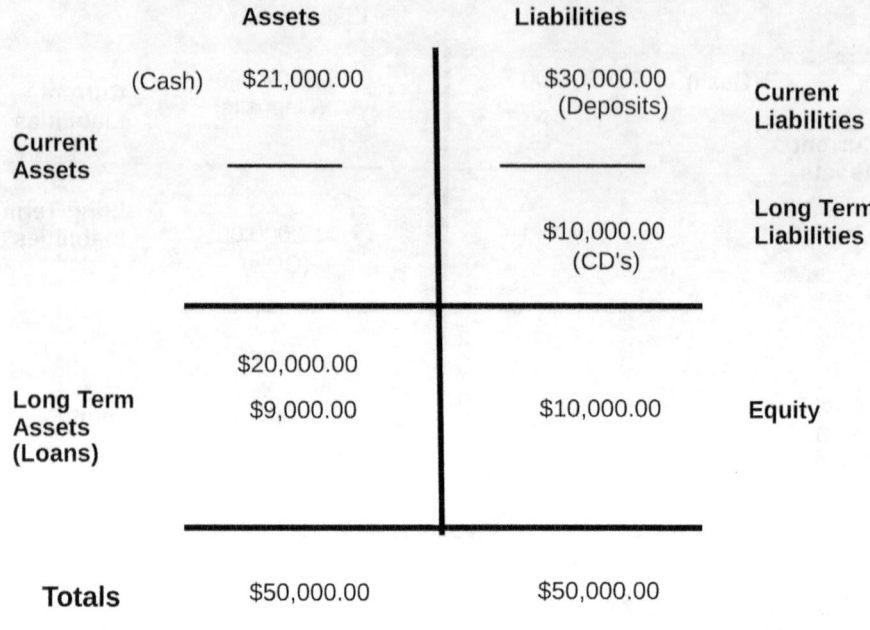

Figure #16

The balance sheet shows a total of $50,000.00 on each side. The asset to equity ratio is now five to one. If you were to divide $50,000.00 into $10,000.00 (total assets into equity), .20 or 20% would be the result, which is the ratio of equity to total assets.

At this point the balance sheet shows the bank has $30,000.00 in deposits and $21,000.00 in cash which means the bank can loan out $18,000.00 in cash leaving $3,000.00 to cover the reserve requirement. Of course this is the beginning of the great juggling act and the multiplier effect of money. If the bank can get all the rest of the loans down the line deposited back in the bank it can loan this $18,000.00 out nine times. This will create $180,000.00 in new loans and deposits and our new balance sheet would look like figure #17 with a total of $230,000.00 at the bottom of each column.

Assets	Liabilities

	Assets	Liabilities	
(Cash)	$21,000.00	$210,000.00 (Deposits)	Current Liabilities
Current Assets	———	———	
		$10,000.00 (CD's)	Long Term Liabilities
Long Term Assets (Loans)	$180,000.00 $20,000.00 $9,000.00	$10,000.00	Equity
Totals	$230,000.00	$230,000.00	

Figure #17

The figure at the bottom of the left hand column is total assets and happens to be 23.0 times larger than the amount of equity. The bank has changed its equity to asset ratio to 4.3%, which is still above the required 3%. Since equity is $10,000.00 total assets can be expanded out to a total of $330,000.00 by bringing in more CD's or deposits. It can also increase its equity through profits or issuing more stock, however, this would also increase the amount of total assets it could have.

Once again we have used an extreme case where all the money from the CD's and equity has been redeposited in the same bank, however, if the money is deposited in another bank it will still increase the money in the system by the multiplier rate. As other banks make loans based on the increase in their equity and new CD's they create, that money, or a good share of it, should end up in your bank, allowing your bank to expand its assets out towards the 3% equity to assets ratio.

Now let us suppose that the bank fell on hard times because the economy went south. Let's also suppose, for the sake of simplicity as well as doing the extreme thing that the $209,000.00 in loans is actually a single home loan and property values have dropped by 25%. If the bank had to sell the $209,000.00 home at a 25% loss due to foreclosure, it would lose $52,250.00 on the sale and would now have an additional $156,750.00 in cash, or total cash of $177,750.00, and its total assets in the left-hand column would now read $177,750.00. This means the right-hand column would need to change by the same amount, and since the demand deposits and loans have not changed, equity is where we must take the $52,250.00 from. This would leave the bank with negative $42,250.00 in equity. The new balance sheet would look like this:

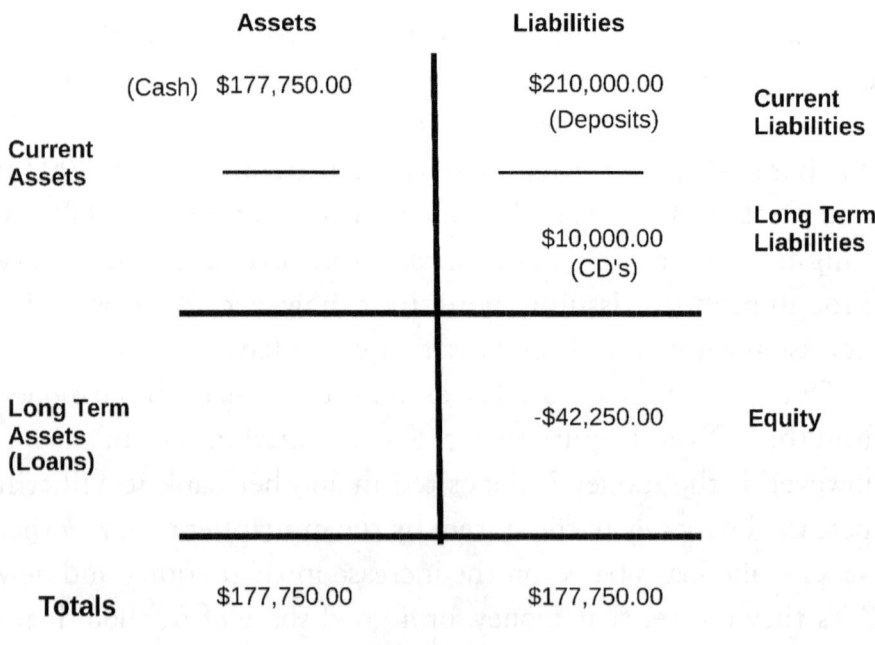

Figure #18

Since the bank has lost all of its equity and more, the Federal Reserve will shut the bank's doors. If the Federal Reserve were to shut the bank's doors and pay off the creditors (deposit and CD holders), the creditors would take a loss of $42,250.00, which on average would be a little under 17% of their money. This is a good example of deleveraging and what it can do to the bank and its creditors, except that the FDIC would bail out most of the creditors if this were a real scenario.

At this point I hope it is clear that your bank must hold 10% of all demand deposits in reserve in cash. It should be equally clear that your bank can leverage its equity, which includes profits, and cash from the loans the bank has taken out as well as equity thirty-three times, not just ten times. It has to maintain at least a 3% equity to asset ratio, which is a leverage rate of just over one to thirty-three. I also hope it is clear what deleveraging can do to a bank.

Looking back to our discussion about how banks own the leveraged assets, the bank will have to pay back demand depositors if the deposits start shrinking. The bank owns its profits and equity, so it does not have to repay this money in the future. However, if the bank is losing money, it has negative profits, or if it has to write off or write down the value of its assets, the write-down usually comes out of equity, which means it has to start deleveraging its equity at the rate of thirty-three to one.

A word about capital: capital and equity are generally the same thing in reference to banking regulation. I mention capital here because there are also additional regulations that involve the word "capital" in place of the word "equity," but capital and equity equate to the same thing. Regulators have broken down assets and equity into several different groupings based on risk and subordination, which allows them to refine the ratio between assets and equity. The point of this book is to show what the multiplier effect is and how it is used by banks. If you understand the equity to assets ratio, you can also understand the capital requirement ratios. The purpose of the various capital ratios is the same as that of the equity to asset ratio: to limit or keep the bank's exposure to risk at some arbitrary level that is deemed manageable by the banks. The arbitrary level of risk is the level at which the depositors and other creditors of the bank appear to be protected from the greed and avarice, real or imagined, of the bankers. Anyone wishing to continue a detailed study of banking will no doubt get into capital ratios, but, for most readers, I feel what we have covered will suffice.

Greed is bad!
It stands to reason that if greed is indeed bad, it should then be done away with.
Unfortunately no form of government ever created has been able to change the hearts of men.
As long as men are, there will be greed!
So if you cannot control the hearts of men, it is sensible to at least regulate their activities!

LOANS AND MORE LOANS

As we have seen, banks can make loans and then turn around and sell them almost immediately. They are making great profits by doing this. Of course they will turn around and use those profits to make more loans, which, in turn, they can immediately sell if they choose to. By doing this profits go off the charts. It is a moneymaking machine without parallel. The truth is that *it doesn't happen!* There are two caveats to the whole process. The first is that in order for the process of creating money through loans to go through the roof, you must have an infinite amount of loans to make. Unfortunately for the banks, there are only so many homes that exist on which they can create loans. The same is true for cars, boats, and farm vehicles and equipment. There are also only so many businesses out there that want or need loans. The bank can sell all its loans, converting those loans into cash, but if there are no more loans to make, the bank is not creating any new assets or profits, only converting the assets it already has into their equivalent in cash, and is left sitting on a pile of cash. The second caveat is that in the United States, the bank's loan to equity ratio cannot exceed 3%. Bank regulation in our country forbids infinite leverage, so there is a limit on how far out banks can leverage their equity in the process of making loans. It is also true that selling loans requires a discount, which the bank will count as a loss that will come out of equity. Reducing your equity is reverse leverage, so it only pushes the bank up against the 3% equity to asset ratio that much faster. Due to regulation banks can't make loans ad infinitum without also increasing their equity ad infinitum.

The banking industry is competitive. Just look at all the banks out there. Living in a capitalistic society, it is reasonable to suppose that a bank's assets may remain constant or even decrease as well as increase in size. If a bank's asset base starts decreasing, the bank may find itself deleveraging. This can happen because the bank loses loans and has to sit on cash, because it has made bad loans that have been written off, or even because of a lack of economic activity. The consequence of sitting on cash is a loss of profits. As long as you are sitting on cash, the cash is not making you any money (profits). The bank can also see a decrease in its assets due to a loss of customers. If the bank loses demand deposits, the amount of money held as cash will start shrinking, and the bank will either have to sell some of its existing loans to increase its cash position or take out loans to cover its cash needs. A bank can lose customers because of competition or because it's geographical area is in decline and people and businesses are moving away. Losing customers because of competition or geographical decline usually happens slowly, and a bank ends up converting its loans to cash with no new loans to make, which allows it to avoid deleveraging as the bank goes into decline. It is also true that the bank can see a decrease in deposits or CDs because the bank is mismanaged.

I also mentioned that a bank's assets could remain static, not increasing or decreasing. In this case a bank's profits tend to stabilize. If a bank's assets are growing, the multiplier effect indicates that its profits will also grow exponentially because of the leveraging. With a stable bank, which is neither increasing nor decreasing, you would expect its assets to stabilize and profits to settle in somewhat lower than if the bank's assets were growing by leaps and bounds.

At this point I hope you realize that in a stable economy, where there is little or no growth or decline, the amount and number of loans would remain more or less unchanged, as would demand deposits. In such a situation, banks, in total, would make all their money from interest and fees and from their ability to turn their loans over quickly or steal market share from the other banks. But in the system as a whole, the amount of money, demand deposits, and loans would remain approximately the same in dollar terms. Money is merely being shuffled around. The velocity of money, or how fast the money turns over, could cause the money supply to increase and rev up the multiplier effect, however, if the economy is stable velocity usually doesn't change significantly.

There is another type of loan that slips in almost unnoticed. Enter the credit card. Each credit card comes with a limit—or at least mine do. This means my bank guarantees me a standing loan of up to the amount of my personal limit. It is mine to use at any time I wish without reservation, to buy anything that does not exceed my credit limit. I have found that I can sometimes exceed the limits on a credit card temporarily, and for a price, but the fact is that the bank wants me to remain under my credit limit.

Of course the bank can leverage these loans, just as it does any other loan. Let us assume that the bank will leverage our credit card debt at the rate of ten to one. If you buy an electronic gizmo at a retail store and you put it on your credit card, the bank only has to cover that purchase by reserving 10% of the purchase price (read loan) in its vaults. The bank can then float the entire purchase as a loan. What you bought is now a part of the great juggling act. If you pay off the balance on your card every month, which, by the way, is a good way to stay financially sound, the bank makes, in cash, 90% of the purchase price of your electronic gizmo. What do you get out of this? Well, if you're smart, your card has no annual fee and you pay no interest. You are free to use the card anytime, anywhere, at no cost to you (the use of the card is free, not the items you purchase), and you don't have to carry cash.

Compare this to a debit card. If you use a debit card to make a purchase, the bank makes nothing. If you have only a debit card, the bank will usually charge you a fee for every purchase you make using the card because that is the only way the bank will make any money. On the other hand, most debit cards can also be used as credit cards. And the bank will even give you cash back or reward points, etcetera, on your monthly statement for using it as a credit card. Using a debit card as a credit card is greatly to the advantage of the bank that issues the debit card. This is true because the debit card, if used as a credit card, will usually be paid from your bank account within three days instead of going on a monthly statement that you will have to pay off at the end of the month. And the bank gets to count it as a loan until it is paid off, which of course helps its profit margin. There are debit cards that don't charge a fee for its use as a debit card because the bank hopes you will use it as a credit card instead.

Any time you use a debit card without using your pin the transaction is counted as if the card were a credit card.

Of course anyone familiar with what goes on behind the scenes in the credit card business knows that credit card companies charge businesses a fee for every credit card and debit card transaction. These fees are paid to several other entities besides the banks, but we are mainly concerned with the banks here. Big businesses can negotiate very low fees, while smaller businesses pay higher fees per transaction. Because the fee payment plan is negotiable, banks can also offer competitive rates and undercut the competition if they desire. These fees are too low to pay for the complete cost of using the card but do pay for some of the cost. The real profit the credit card company makes is from the use of the multiplier effect.

If I don't pay off my card every month but choose to carry a balance, I end up paying a healthy interest rate. No credit card company can survive on less than about 25% interest. It would take that much money to keep track of every transaction and send you a statement every month and keep the great juggling act supported. Between fees and interest, a credit card company is probably just making ends meet, if that. Yet the cards that carry a balance are the bread and butter base for the credit card industry. The credit card company is making interest plus part of the principal every month. Monthly payments on the principle, though it might not be much, probably accounts for a substantial part of its profits. Suppose for hypothetical purposes that 50% of a credit card company's cardholders are carrying balances and making payments in a timely manner. These balances are leveraged. Any principle paid off is producing a profit that is the result of the leverage. Of its remaining cardholders, 25% are paying their cards off every month, and 25% are not making their payments or just barely making payments, with a 20%-plus interest rate. On average, if you count just the individuals who pay off their monthly balances and those in or near default, the credit card company would probably just break even. If it can increase the numbers of cardholders who pay their cards off every month, its profits go up. If, at the same time, it can decrease the number of cardholders who are in default, its profits will go up even more. For those card holders near default but still making payments, their high interest rates and small payments on principle, which is leveraged, are making the bank good money. Also if the bank can increase its total assets, those card holders carrying a balance, or leverage its money out further, it can make more profits. Banks that offer credit cards and administer them properly make very good money.

Let me ask a question. Can you think of any reason why banks would not want to put a credit card in the hands of every man, woman, and child in the world, barring the slight chance that they might not be able to make their payments? There is money in the credit card business, and the more customers you have, the more money you can make, as long as the cardholders make their payments.

As I described earlier, banks eventually hit a barrier where there are no loans to be had at any price. In the last several decades, banks seem to have become progressively greedier. Since there are only so many loans to be had, the banks started looking for added ways to loan out more money.

Back when I was young, leaving home, going to college, and venturing out into the world on my own, things were different. It was hard to get a credit card; you had to ask and keep asking. Credit card companies were also rather stingy about large credit limits. Today credit card offers come in the mail all the time without us asking and with the promise of prequalification and high credit limits.

When I was young, if you wanted to buy a home, the bank would require that you put up 20% of either the sales price or the appraised value of the home yourself, and the bank would make a loan on only 80% of the appraised value of the home. If you happened to be a veteran approved for a Veterans Affairs loan or could qualify for a Federal Housing Administration loan, you could get a loan for 95% to 98% of the appraised value of the home. But most folks back then had to put up 20% of the appraised value of the home. The 20% was the bank's guarantee that you wouldn't walk away from the mortgage, or if by chance the property lost value, the homeowner would bear the first 20% of the devaluation. Even if the housing market went down, it would have to go down more than 20% before the bank would lose money if the bank had to repossess the home and resell it.

I can still recall the era right before the financial crisis of 2008, when home equity loans were being offered for 100% of the appraised value of the home. Some outfits even offered to loan out 125% of the appraised value of the home. Those were heady speculative days. Banks had run up against the loan barrier and were trying to expand the size of loans. If, for instance, you could loan out that extra 20% that the bank originally required as security from the homeowner, the total potential loan market would grow by 20% of the value of all extant home loans where the owners had had to put up 20% of the values of the homes. That is a huge potential market. The same would be true if the banks could make loans on 125% of the appraised values of all the homes on the market.

At the same time, banks were finding creative ways to finance homes so they could qualify more people for loans. They came up with crazy balloon payments or interest rates that increased as the loans matured. The concept was that inflation would continue, wages would continue to rise, and asset prices would also go up. Then, starting sometime before the financial crisis, everything reversed direction and only got worse afterward.

Banks were also looking for new and different ways to make more profits and find more money. One such idea was to package mortgages in bundles and sell those packages as unsecured bonds. When I first heard of mortgage bonds, I thought the banks were selling the houses twice. If the bonds were indeed secured by offering the home and property as collateral, they would indeed have been selling the same house twice. However, the bonds were unsecured, so it was not the same thing as selling the house twice. On the other hand, it was creating a debt instrument on top of another debt instrument. If the bank were to sell the mortgage outright, the bank would be paid off, and there would still be only one financial instrument attached to the house. By selling mortgage bonds, the bank still owns the mortgage and its income stream, and it also receives the money that it would have received if it had sold the mortgage. It is a little like having your cake and eating it too. Of course it has to repay the bonds down the road, but it now has extra money to loan or invest. Loans will be leveraged; whereas investments would only make interest or appreciation in value. If its loans and investment of the money it makes on the sale of the bond is wise, it will be able to pay back the mortgage bonds and still make a nice profit. On the other hand, if it invests the money from the bonds poorly, they will end up with one income stream supporting two financial instruments: one financial instrument that is a debt against the bank's future income and one that is supposed to provide the bank with an income. If the economy turns south, as it did it in 2008, it does not leave banks that own mortgage bonds looking very pretty.

Bonds are loans and as a financial instrument they can be bought and sold much like stocks on the stock market, but they are loans. My explanation of a mortgage bond was highly simplified and I will treat them a little more in depth in the chapter on Bonds and Swaps that comes later in the book. There are three things about bonds that are attached to mortgages that you need to keep straight: someone must own the mortgages, someone has to manage the mortgages (collect payments and deposit them, make sure the insurance and property taxes are paid and collect on delinquencies), and last someone has to pay the interest on the bond (loan). More on bonds later.

In the end, as individuals running the banks have gotten greedier, the banks have looked for creative ways to expand their assets (loans), which has significantly increased the risk the banks face.

It is also a little unfair to blame everything on the greed of bankers, there were other factors involved in the lead up to the financial crisis. One of those factors was misplaced regulation by the federal government.

Fannie Mae and Freddie Mac are two entities that are owned by shareholders and not by the government. However, it is said that they are sponsored by the government. They were chartered by Congress. For this reason they are called government-sponsored enterprises (GSE's). The government sponsored them by backing them financially and allowing them to borrow money from the 'treasury at rates that were generally below market and they could also get tax relief from some state and local taxes. They would buy mortgages singly or in bundles from banks who originated the mortgages. (We discussed why banks would sell a loan in a previous chapter). By sponsoring the secondary mortgage market it helped keep cash and thus credit flowing through the banks.

Freddie and Fannie had strict standards about what kind of loans they would accept. They wanted 10-20% down payments and a record of past payments that were on time, which meant they usually only bought a mortgage after it had been in place for a year or more. There had to be a valid credit report on the home buyer that met certain criteria and the home buyer had to have a debt-to-income ratio sufficient to imply that they were financially stable. They were some of the biggest players in the secondary mortgage market and helped set and insure the standards for loans.

Because Freddie and Fannie were chartered by Congress, Congress felt like they could direct how they operated in the market place. In 1992, after many complaints, Congress passed the "affordable housing goals" for the two entities. The complaint was that the industry standards for obtaining a mortgage were so high that low and moderate-income families could not afford to buy a home and thus were missing out on the American dream. Congress directed the two entities to make 30% of their total purchases from home buyers in the low to middle income bracket, as defined by the median income in the community that the home buyer lived in. Congress also determined that Fannie and Freddie could lower the down payment required on a mortgage to below 5% without reducing the quality of the mortgage (increasing the risk of default). Congress also gave oversight of the directive to the Department of Housing and Urban Development (HUD) with the ability to raise the percentage of loans that the two entities would have to accept. Accordingly, HUD raised the percentage over the years until in 2008 they were required to buy at least 56% of their mortgages from low and middle income families. HUD was clearly trying to get the market to lower its underwriting standards. In order to meet this goal Freddie and Fannie were eventually purchasing mortgages with no down payments and poor credit histories. Freddie and Fannie were clearly into the subprime mortgage market.

As the biggest entities in the secondary market, they were setting the standards and many other purchasers in the secondary market followed suit because it is a competitive market. Most observers felt that since Freddie and Fannie were GSE's they were backed by the federal government and thus the loans they were purchasing were guaranteed by the government, unfortunately that really wasn't the case. Many of the subprime loans that had been bought went bust and the Federal government had to pump billions of dollars into Freddie and Fannie to keep them solvent even though the government hadn't guaranteed the mortgages.

At this point I don't think many people need me to tell them where this all ended. The real point is that when the government starts meddling in the market, telling businesses how to run their business, they can really mess things up. Regulation is supposed to keep the players in the market honest, not tell them how to do their business. Good regulation will encourage honesty, transparency and openness while leaving the market free to do its thing.

Being observant putting two and two together,
and reading between the lines,
especially accurately reading between the lines,
are human qualities that escape nearly everyone
at least part of the time
and most of us most of the time!

SOME IMPLICATIONS OF THE MULTIPLIER EFFECT OF MONEY

There are perhaps a number of outcomes implied by the multiplier effect of money. They may be so obvious that we don't even see them. The first implication is debt, and debt is so obvious we almost over look its importance. Debt is a serious part of the multiplier effect of money; in fact the multiplier effect wouldn't exist if it weren't for debt. Trading demand deposits for longer-term debt is the working mechanism of the multiplier effect. There are some very well-intentioned individuals who would like to see all debt done away with or at least written off. But if any of us wishes to own a home, we probably wouldn't have the means to do it without the help of a loan from a bank. Even buying a car would be beyond the immediate means of many people. Banks offer loans as a service because we need the money if we wish to purchase big-ticket items. We can't live without banks; neither can banks live without us. In the end the world's money supplies and all that depends upon those money supplies are tied to debt. Debt is almost universal in the developed world. Debt is what keeps great economies going. At the same time, giving in to debt can be a little like giving in to the "dark side"; it can destroy or enslave you. Debt is a two-edged sword that should be kept sheathed and handled carefully when brandished. This applies equally to nations as well as to individuals or businesses.

Another obvious implication that runs parallel to the first is the fact that our money, currency, is based on debt. At least 90% of the money out there is only there on paper. It was created out of thin air and exists because of the debt instruments, mortgages and loans that were created. If we were to suddenly do away with all that debt, we would probably lose 90% of all the money in our economy. The result might not be obvious, but I will deal with this subject in another chapter. So if you don't see what is coming down the road when you lose 90% of the money in the economy, hang in there, and we will get to it soon enough. The important thing to understand is that our money as well as its supply is based on debt. Debt is what underwrites—is the very foundation—of our money supply and our economy!

One implication we have already established is that the creation of money through the multiplier effect creates a good deal of wealth for the banks and their owners. Banks take serious risks and deserve to make good money from doing so. They also need to shoulder those risks if they mismanage them or they really aren't taking any risks at all, and if you don't bear the risk, you shouldn't get the reward. Perhaps it would be better to say that if they don't have to shoulder the risks, it is because they are able to pass those risks on to someone else, which is simply not fair. Once the risk is created, fortunately or unfortunately, someone will eventually reap the reward for success or failure. And if you believe in free enterprise, the free market, or capitalism, those reaping either reward, good or bad, should be those creating the risks.

Another implication has to do with leverage. We discussed leverage in a previous chapter; however, leverage is as much about profits as it is about ratios, equity or assets. It is easy to overlook the profit as we discuss the principles behind leverage and its calculation. The bank is making interest and principle of up to nine times the cash reserve and thirty three times the equity.

Another implication is the idea of a need for a safety net. If banks leverage money at the rate of ten to one or greater, they create not only wealth but also a lot of risk. The great juggling act is indeed risky, and it requires managers and owners who understand how to live and deal with the risk. On the other hand, it is also convenient when there is someone out there who can mitigate the risk and bail the bank out if the bank falls on hard times through no fault of its own (mismanagement is a fault). Most banks that make bad decisions are allowed to go under. Their owners and creditors are allowed to lose their money. On the other hand, some banks are so big that they would destabilize the banking industry in a significant part of the economy and are therefore not allowed to go under. In times of crisis, like the financial crisis of 2007–2008, the Federal Reserve bailed out the whole banking system. That is its job. In this case it even bailed out some businesses in conjunction with the federal government. There are times when it is worth it to save the entire nation. The real hope is that it will eventually be able to recover all the money it has pumped into the economy, businesses, and banks. The Federal Reserve is, generally speaking, a good safety net and may be necessary. By dissolving bad banks efficiently, the Federal Reserve can perhaps save the world from the banks that misuse the multiplier effect of money.

Another implication that is probably obvious but ought to be stated clearly is the idea of overreach. Simply stated, overreach is usually spelled "greed." If banks try to leverage too far or too far too fast, or simply try to find their way around regulations so they can extend their risks and thus their profits, it is and should be called mismanagement. When a bank becomes so big and diversified into foreign accounts and governments and business and derivatives and equities as well as other things, it is simply too big to fail. In the eyes of the regulators, being too big to fail has, in many cases, become an excuse for allowing those banks to be mismanaged. Overreach typically requires regulation of banks by some outside institution and should be applicable to all banks.

Another implication is that banks are the main engine behind our economy. Economic growth within a country requires a number of factors. Real economic growth requires that most of the citizens within a country have a strong work ethic and drive, which has to do with productivity. Another is creativity, imagination, or vision that will create new means of production as well as products. Still another is strong moral values; if no one is honest, including the regulators, you can't expect great things over the long haul. Yet another is opportunity. Opportunity does not exist without freedom, and the more freedom there is, the more opportunity seems to abound. Last of those I will mention is the money or wealth, usually called capital, to make it all happen, which depends in large measure on strong banks. Arguably you could say that if any of these items are missing in an economy, that economy would be seriously hindered.

While banks can seriously misuse the multiplier effect of money, they can expand the money supply within an economy by at least ten times, which will free up business to increase their activities by at least ten times, or so the theory goes. This makes the multiplier effect of money a huge engine that fuels the needs of an ever-expanding economy.

Historically the Islamic societies of the Middle East and North Africa were some of the most advanced societies in the world, more advanced than Europe. But there came a time when the economies and sciences of Europe and the West far out-stripped the rest of the world, including the Islamic nations. Many economists have pointed to the Protestant work ethic and said it was one of the main reasons for the change. Still others have indicated that it was the formation of democracies and the opportunities that were associated with individual freedom. In recent times, with increased understanding of Islamic law, it has also become apparent that Islamic law doesn't allow the use of many financial techniques that are used in the West, including the multiplier effect of money. Without the ability to expand money and their economies with it, they were simply left behind. The multiplier effect of money creates an economic engine that leaves all other systems in the dust.

Moving forward requires that we make choices.
The rewards and punishments that follow all our choices
will be ours to enjoy or regret,
remember or forget, and even learn from.

RISK

I once read a blurb somewhere that claimed to be a parable. It went, "Yea behold the turtle…he goeth nowhere save he first thrusteth forth his neck." Please forgive the old English and the fact that the parable is not religious. The author was trying to say two things: If a turtle doesn't stick its head out of its shell, it will never go anywhere; and second, if you don't stick your neck out—thus taking the chance of having your head cut off at the neck—you can never achieve much! Sticking your neck out there where someone can take a whack at it becomes the defining essence of risk and the rewards associated with that risk.

Risks can be small to the point of inconsequence or great to the point of destruction of much of humanity. Environmental groups and others have pointed out that the world and humanity might be destroyed if we don't control pollution, and they may even be right. The point I'm trying to make is that risks can range from very small to huge. Every choice we make involves some kind of risk. It may only be a lost opportunity because we choose to do something different and lose the opportunity, but we all live with risk. Some risks are calculated; some are only guessed at; some unforeseen, while others are ignored. Some rewards for our actions appear to be so great that our desire to take the action required will allow no risk, regardless of how great, to get in our way. We each live with risk; it is unavoidable. Someone said, "Life is a chance," and we should live and enjoy the chance or risk.

Sometimes we live as though the risks we take will only affect us: "it is my decision and I'm the only one who will get hurt." Unfortunately man leaves his footprint on relationships as well as his environment. Relationships include those with friends, family, coworkers, and to a lesser extent others who associate with them. Environment includes our neighborhood, place of education, work, natural resources, nation, and world. Our influence can be huge, and the risks we take can move through everything and everyone around us and beyond.

Around the time of the Great Depression, financial leveraging had become such a problem that Congress decided to limit leveraging in many different ways. One way was that credit unions and savings and loans could not use the multiplier effect of money. In effect members of those institutions pooled their savings together, and members could then borrow the cash to buy a home or car or washing machine. But all the money the institution had to loan out was the cash in its vaults. There were a limited number of loans it could make. As those loans were paid back every month, with interest, the pool of cash would increase until another loan could be made. Getting a loan was a slow process, but it was secure. The savings and loan owned whatever was bought until it was paid off, and it also owned your deposits. An individual's deposits and loans were totally committed, and profits were shared. For every $1 or $5 in savings, the depositor was credited with one share in the institution. Profits were divided among shareholders according to the number of shares you held. If you defaulted on your loan, the institution sold your property, and any loss from the sale was covered by your deposits or shared by the other shareholders on an equal basis. If the sale of your property produced a profit, you kept your savings and got your share of the profits. In many ways these institutions were more like cooperatives than banks. The idea was to regulate the industry and create nearly risk-free institutions to protect people's homes and other property from catastrophic loss (risk).

Since the financial crisis in 2008, banking regulators around the world have been seeking to limit the risks the banks can take. Because of the nature of the great recession itself, many banks have had to retrench on their own volition and seek to limit their exposure to risks. Basel III is a set of voluntary rules determined by an organization known as the Basel Committee on Banking Supervision that sets guidelines for banks in a non-compulsory way. In other words banks don't have to follow the Basel guidelines, but regulators tend to take the Basel recommendations seriously. In the United States, Congress created the Dodd-Frank Wall Street Reform and Consumer Protection Act and it became law in July 2010, which regulates the financial industry more heavily than a lot of financial institutions would like. It is easy to see that the banks are to blame for the financial and economic mess we are in. The banks use the multiplier effect of money and face the risks involved. Yet the banks could not do it unless investors and ordinary people were willing to buy into services the financial institutions were offering. People need to understand how banks and the multiplier effect work and the risks involved. If they don't, they will never have the information needed to govern themselves and financial institutions.

As I mentioned in the last chapter, the Islamic world of the Middle East and North Africa was left behind in part because they couldn't use the multiplier effect of money. The risk involved in the multiplier effect allows an economy to expand. Of course it can backfire, but where risk is great, the rewards can also be huge. And to most people, the advantages of a modern economy seem worth the risk.

When I was just a kid, I loved cartoons. I can remember the portrayal of the ostrich being pursued by someone or something and the ostrich sticking its head in the sand in alarm. It was so obviously stupid to react in that way, but ostriches will be ostriches. Unfortunately many humans try to do the same thing at various times in their lives. We live in a world filled with risks, and we cannot avoid them. Getting out of bed in the morning opens our life to risks. But staying in bed with covers pulled up over our heads puts us at risk because we are doing nothing. If you do nothing, your body and mind as well as your resources atrophy. Generally speaking we don't learn much by hiding in our beds either. Life moves on and we are left behind. If we aren't out there struggling to get ahead or at least keep up, we become outdated and are left behind. The challenges of life provide us with risk, and if we accept the risk and try to manage the risk, the effort can produce rewards as well as pain. We may not like risk, but we can't live without it.

In the context of finance, the banks pose serious risks, but without those risks our economy would still be as regressive as the economies of the Islamic countries that were left in the Middle Ages. The risks are part of the great engine behind our modern economies.

In many ways we all live with risk, and, in truth, without taking risk we would be like the turtle that refuses to stick its head out of its shell. Without risk there is little real progress we can make, and without taking risk we cannot make a profit from our creativity, initiative, and industry. Risk is one of those things that helps make the world go around for each of us, and there are rewards in being able to manage the risks we face.

Reality does not necessarily have anything to do with
the world you or I think we live in!

THE REAL WORLD

We each live in two worlds simultaneously. This may seem strange, but it is true. We each have a personal world that we live in. In our personal worlds, we have friends, family, and other individuals with whom we have relationships. We live and work within certain environments and have our daily and yearly routines. Everything we are and whatever we do, participate in, and have control of, and even who we know and associate with, makes up our personal world. The other world we live in is the wider world over which we have no influence and sometimes no understanding or knowledge. There is in all probability an individual who has lived on Manhattan Island all his life and never been off the island. Yet, out there beyond Manhattan, there is the rest of the state, the United States, and the world. Perhaps you don't live on Manhattan Island but, maybe you have never left the land of your nativity. In addition to where you have never been there are also governments, NGOs, and large corporations. We get a lot of petroleum from places I've never been. There are things going on in the rest of the world beyond our range of experience that affect our lives in ways that we don't understand and sometimes don't even recognize. Some of those influences are miniscule, like the size of next year's world coffee bean crop, which will make the cost of a pound of coffee go up or down a few cents, while others can be very huge, like a serious shortage of petroleum.

I have been explaining how banks function, as well as why. I hope that some of the examples I have given are familiar to you in the world in which you live and that they explain to some extent why some of the things you experience are what they are. If I were to tell you everything in this book, yet they didn't jive with what you experience in your personal world, you would be right to question it. If it does jive with some of the things going on in your personal world, I hope the rest of the ideas will be enlightening and of some value to you in making decisions about how to deal with your world. Even so I have been telling you things that may seem totally unbelievable because they are so foreign to your personal world. Sometimes the real world out there is as strange to us as our world would seem if one of our ancestors from two hundred years ago were to suddenly be plopped down in our living room that represents our personal reality. Reality is not always what we think it to be, nor is our reality always defined by the rest of the world, but the more we learn and know about the wider world, the more informed and full our lives should become.

I have obviously used extremes, ad infinitum, in this book for the obvious purpose of clarity, but the real world is not nearly so extreme, so I hope you will forgive my usage of extremes.

A balance sheet is also at times unrealistic in the study of a business. A balance sheet is in reality a snapshot of the financial position of a company taken at a precise moment in time, and the snapshot does not change with the company's ongoing business. The real balance sheet would change every time a financial transaction of any kind took place. The balance sheet would be in constant flux, which may represent reality, but dealing with a balance sheet that is constantly changing is also not realistic. At the end of the day, the Federal Reserve and your bank both close their books, and the balance sheet remains frozen until business starts again the next day. In reality the reserve requirement for a bank would change with every financial transaction at the bank. Because it would be impossible to change the reserve requirement with every financial transaction, the Federal Reserve sets the reserve requirement for a bank only once every two weeks. Letting the bank's reserve requirement remain fixed for up to fourteen days can be both good and bad, but it is preferable to the costs associated with hitting a moving target.

The real world out there and the reality of our personal world are not necessarily the same thing. Learning to distinguish between the two requires that we expand our horizons. In learning of the greater world we will perhaps learn better how to deal with both.

In the real world, banks play an important part in both our personal world and in the much larger world beyond. This book is meant to take you into that larger world and illustrate how detrimental banks can be to the world at large because of their use of the multiplier effect; however, banks have provided us with much of what we have materially. Banks are the engine behind our economy and therefore can be equally as beneficial as detrimental.

Sometimes taking a journey out into the world beyond our own personal reality can be a scary thing and other times a very welcome excursion. Other times a journey out of our personal reality can be accomplished by as little as reading a new book or surfing the Internet, looking for something specific that has pricked our awareness. In either case, be the journey emotionally harrowing or exhilarating, we each have the opportunity to expand our horizons and gain a better understanding of the greater world in which we live.

The bottom line is that I hope this book has helped you understand your personal world a little better and at the same time has taken you out into the broader world, where you have also learned some things you did not know.

PART 2

*Now that we have tackled the
multiplier effect of money
and how banks use it, it is time
to turn our attention
to more dismal economic details:
details like expansion of the money supply,
inflation and deflation,
and how the Federal Reserve Bank,
as well as the multiplier effect of money,
is complicit in all of this.*

In the United States, Congress has responsibility to regulate
the minting of coin and printing or issuing of paper money.
Is leaving this responsibility to politicians and the political process a
good thing?
Whether or not anyone likes it, Congress has transferred that authority
to the technocrat professionals at the Federal Reserve Bank.

EXPANSION OF THE MONEY SUPPLY

Expansion of the money supply is a fancy way of saying the government has rolled out the printing presses and is printing money. Yet the government really isn't printing money and putting it into circulation. Most governments, which use the tool of actually printing money and putting it into circulation, use printed money to pay the governments bills directly or to pay off government loans in cash, thus putting the money into circulation. This is not what is happening in the United States when we talk about expanding the money supply.

The first clarification ought to be about the role, or at least part of the role, of the Federal Reserve Bank. The Federal Reserve Board and Bank System was created by Congress and was delegated the responsibility to be the sole seller of United States government securities, to regulate the supply of money, and to oversee the issuance of new money in the form of coins and bills. The Federal Reserve Board and Banks oversee the mints and the printing presses and sells the securities, doing all the legwork for the Treasury Department. All of these duties are now out of the hands of politicians. Good or bad, that is the way it is. Congress can regulate the Federal Reserve System or even revoke its charter if it wishes to. The Federal Reserve Board and Banks function within the laws that Congress has created for the regulation of its activities. I hope we are clear about this. There are, no doubt, many individuals who feel the Federal Reserve System's powers are too broad, but the Federal Reserve System tries to live within the bounds set by Congress.

We should note a couple of other facts. The Federal Reserve System is a two-headed beast. The first head is the Federal Reserve Board or Board of Governors, located in Washington, DC. The Federal Reserve Board is independent, as much as possible, of both banks and government. The Federal Reserve Board makes decisions about the money supply and other monetary policies. Please understand that this is an abbreviated and simplified list of the Federal Reserve Board's responsibilities. The governing board of the Federal Reserve is appointed by the president of the United States but serves without interference from the president or Congress.

The second head of the beast is the twelve district branches of the Federal Reserve. Each branch is responsible for the regulation of the banks within its geographical district. Regulation has many forms, and again this is short and simplified. Within the districts are two classes of banks: retail and commercial. Retail banks deal exclusively with individuals and their needs. Commercial banks deal with businesses. Some banks have different branches or divisions within the bank, some divisions doing retail banking and others commercial. The district branches of the Federal Reserve issue stock to the commercial banks in their districts, and you could conclude that each of the Federal Reserve

Bank districts is therefore owned by the commercial banks within its boundaries. The banks in the district choose the majority of the board members that controls the district's decisions and actions. The Federal Reserve Board appoints some of the district board members, which gives the Federal Reserve Board some oversight and control within the districts. The district board is similar to a board of trustees or directors of a corporation. The Federal Reserve branch banks handle the day-to-day functioning of the Federal Reserve Banking system and regulation of banks, while the Federal Reserve Board handles and oversees the functions associated with major policy and monetary decisions.

Accordingly the Federal Reserve Board decides when and by how much to expand the money supply. The Federal Reserve Board increases or decreases the money supply by buying or selling US securities and other bonds through the Open Market Committee, which operates in the bond market. The Open Market Committee is composed of the Federal Reserve Bank branch presidents and a number of the governors of the Federal Reserve Board and makes the decisions concerning monetary policy. Increasing or decreasing the money supply is a monetary policy. The Open Market Committee has its own staff, which performs all of the committee's operations, including the purchase and sale of bonds. These operations sound quite simple but are really quite complicated.

When the Federal Reserve Board's Open Market Committee sells securities in the bond market, it is taking money out of the system (economy). People are turning their money over to the Federal Reserve Board in exchange for bonds. When the Open Market Committee buys bonds, it is putting money back into the market (economy). The Federal Reserve Board is giving money to the bondholders in exchange for bonds. If the bonds have appreciated in value before the Open Market Committee buys them, the sale of the bond puts a little bit more money into the economy because of the increase in value of the bonds. The amount of the increase is not huge, but it is an increase. Of course that small amount of money will eventually be multiplied through the multiplier effect. If the Federal Reserve Board reverses the process or sells bonds, it is taking money out of the economy, and the money supply decreases, eventually, in accordance with the multiplier effect. By going through this process, the Federal Reserve Board doesn't have to print money to increase the money supply. The staff at the Open Market Committee's headquarters in New York buys and sells bonds nearly every day the market is open. Controlling the money supply is an ongoing saga, and the Federal Reserve Board does what it does in accordance with the wishes and oversight of Congress and through the Open Market Committee.

The Federal Reserve Board can also increase the money supply by lowering the interest rate it charges for overnight loans. With lower interest rates on overnight loans, banks are supposed to feel like borrowing money is cheap enough that it is in their interest to expand their leverage of money as far as they can, thus increasing the amount of money in the system. If the banks do indeed take the bait, their leverage against equity increases, the great juggling act gets a little bigger, and the bank may have to obtain more money in the form of overnight loans. The idea is that if the interest rates are lower, the bankers will be more willing to expand their leverage, which increases the money supply.

This process is one of trickle-down economics. The Federal Reserve Board buys bonds on the open market or decreases the interest rate on overnight loans, allowing banks to create money that is loaned out to businesses, and businesses in turn expand their production and hire more people. Expanding the money supply is not about printing money but rather about allowing the banks to use the multiplier effect to increase the money supply after the Federal Reserve Board has decreased interest rates or purchased bonds

This leaves us begging for a reason why the money supply needs to be expanded in the first place. There are at least three good reasons to increase the money supply. The first has to do with expanding the economy, which translates into the Federal Reserve Board's actually trying to keep the economy growing. The second reason is the idea that as the economy expands, the economy's money supply must grow with it, or money will be in short supply and the economy will become slightly depressed. The third reason is similar to the second reason. If the velocity of money revs up, the money supply increases all on its own and more cash needs to be injected into the system to meet the reserve requirements resulting from the increase in money and its being deposited with the banks. This increase in cash can be handled by the Federal Reserve Board buying bonds with cash, and thus there is more cash in the economy, which will allow banks to hold it as reserve requirements. The first and second reasons are different because with the second one, the Federal Reserve Board is trying to expand the money supply within an economy that is already expanding, and with the first, the Federal Reserve Board is trying to increase the money supply to expand an economy that is either not growing or merely growing very slowly. An explanation of the second reason requires some development, and I will take care of that in the next chapter, but for now we will have to let the answer ride. The third reason is very similar to the second: the Federal Reserve Board is trying to catch up with an economy expanding due to velocity rather than the increases in labor and business due to loans. An increase in velocity is generally caused by consumers increasing their spending, which amounts to a bottom up increase in the size of the economy rather than a trickle down expansion of the economy.

Keeping the economy growing, which is the first reason I gave for expanding the money supply, is a little reminiscent of the carrot and stick approach to things. It is like the old analogy where the driver of the donkey cart, in an effort to get the cart moving, dangles a carrot from a stick out in front of the donkey. The donkey, seeing the carrot in front of him, walks forward to try to reach the carrot, and thus the cart is put in motion. It is also similar to the trickle-down effect that we discussed earlier, where commercial banks make loans to businesses and those businesses expand their activities and product lines and hire more people, buy more materials from suppliers, and sell more products. With our country's growing population, young people come out of college looking for jobs, and if the economy isn't growing, there are no jobs for them, or for others who may have been displaced from the workforce. Keeping the economy growing to accommodate new workers is a great boon to the wealth and stability of a nation. Expanding the money supply also keeps interest rates low, which encourages businesses and individuals to take out loans. I explained earlier how interest rates are established by supply and demand. If the Federal Reserve Board expands the money supply, there is usually a greater supply of money than demand, so the interest rate remains low, which encourages businesses to borrow more money.

By the prudent use of monetary policy, the Federal Reserve Board can—or at least tries to—keep the economy expanding. Somewhere along the line, economists came to the conclusion that increasing the money supply by about 2% each year will—or at least should—keep the economy of a nation growing at a modest but consistent rate. The Federal Reserve Board is playing with a huge free market economy, and the economy can be very fickle, to say the least. But the Federal Reserve Board takes its mission seriously and does the best it can. Of course the Federal Reserve Board is run by humans, and after all is said and done, humans are humans, and even the best are blindsided or misjudge the effects of the things they do. Sometimes the Federal Reserve Board and other central banks even get caught on new turf where they have never been before. In using the multiplier effect to expand the money supply, they are wielding a two-edged sword, and the Federal Reserve Board sometimes finds itself swinging a little blindly if not also wildly. For my part I can honestly say I don't know of any man or set of men who could do a better job than the current ones. Sometimes it has only a wing and a prayer to operate on at the very best.

In conclusion, there are good reasons to expand the money supply, and the Federal Reserve Board has tools at its disposal that it uses to do so, as well as expand the economy of our nation, and most of those tools are used in conjunction with the multiplier effect of money.

When things change, and they always do,
there are always winners and losers!

WINNERS AND LOSERS

We need to go back. Actually, in going back through the chapters I discovered I never have drawn this picture. What you see below is a reservoir of money in a jar. The jar contains all the money in our country's economy. You can see that at the bottom of the jar is the 10% cash reserve held by banks, and above that is the other 90% of the money supply, which exists on paper only.

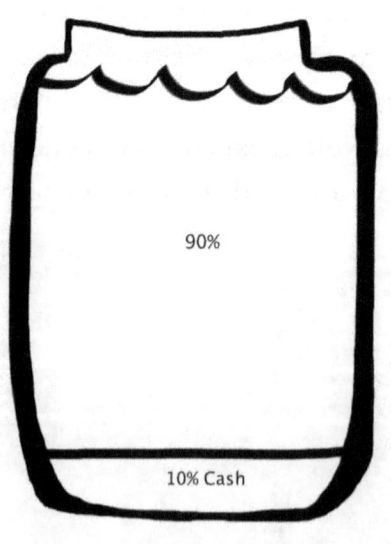

Figure #19
Drawing by Aubrey Benincosa

This is a simple illustration, but one which we will alter as we go. Dollar amounts don't matter at this point—only the percentage of cash and the percent of money created out of thin air. Please understand that we will be talking in extremes, so I hope you understood the intent of the chapter on extremes.

In theory the amount of money in the jar represents the total amount of money in the economy, and you could say that all of the money transactions in the economy are transacted with the money that is in the jar. Every item bought in a grocery store, every home bought or sold, every toy, every book, every cruise on a ship or flight on a plane—everything is bought with the money in the jar. The velocity with which this money turns over makes even more money, but the concept of the money in the jar includes all the money in the economy regardless of the velocity.

We also introduce supply and demand at his point. In the supply and demand equation, there is also price and risk. We will suppose—an extreme—that there is no risk involved, and this leaves us with the mathematical formula Price = Demand / Supply. Actually the formula ought to look more like this:

$$New\ Price = Old\ Price\ (Demand\ /\ Supply)$$

Supply and demand are kind of relative. It is difficult to equate them to actual numbers; however, the significance of the equation is that if demand (the numerator) is larger than supply (the denominator), you get a fraction that is greater than one, and by multiplying the old price by a fraction greater than one, the price will go up. If supply is greater than demand, the fraction will be less than one, and the new price will go down. Simply put, if the supply is greater than demand, the price of the item being supplied will fall until the price is so low that other individuals step in and start buying the item, which will bring demand to a point where it not only meets but exceeds the supply, and the price begins to come up until equilibrium is achieved between supply and demand. The other side of the coin is that if supply is less than demand, prices will go up until certain people can no longer afford the item being supplied or are no longer willing to buy the item at the given price, at which point demand falls to equal the supply, at the current price. In the equilibrium of the free market, where supply equals demand, price is established through trial and error, and equilibrium can change on an ongoing basis, even on a daily or hourly basis for some goods and services. Of course the free market doesn't do math, which means that the price in the market is not determined by science, math, but rather by the intuition, guesswork, perception, or a slick sale due to the abilities of *all* the participants in the market. The market is said to be dynamic rather than static. The market moves and flows and changes for what often appears to be no reason at all.

Going back to our jar, assume that the amount of money in the jar suddenly increases by the extreme amount of 100%. Now the supply of money in the jar is twice the original amount of money. If this change happened overnight, the next morning everyone in the economy would have twice the amount of money with which to make purchases. You might think this a crazy scenario, but a very similar thing has been happening in the Islamic world. When the autocratic governments in the Middle East and other Islamic countries, who have deep pockets due to their petroleum reserves, saw what was happening with the recent uprisings in the Arab world, known as the Arab Spring, suddenly they started handing out significantly larger amounts of money to the people on state welfare and government subsidies and to government employees in an attempt to keep them happy and prevent them from revolting in favor of a more democratic government. In most cases the changes happened more or less overnight. It is very similar to the example that I am demonstrating, though not quite as extreme, because the increase in most cases weren't 100% of what they had before. In my example, with twice as much money to spend, everyone goes on a spending spree, and supplies start to fall rapidly because demand went up very quickly and exceeds supply. The prices of the goods being bought will rise until supply and demand reach equilibrium. In theory equilibrium will be reached when the price of goods double because there is exactly twice as much money. At double the price, the equilibrium is the same as it was with only half the amount of money in the jar. The only thing that will change in the end is that the price will double. This is a very simple example of monetary inflation. In the real world a lot of the money handed out in the Islamic countries could have been spent on things other than goods and services in their economy; examples could include repaying debt, taxes, buying a product directly from China rather than locally or even saving the extra money. Let us look at the opposite of this example. Overnight the money supply shrinks by 50%. The very next morning, people wake up, and suddenly they only have half as much money to spend on everything they need and want. They will only be able to buy so much, and supply will be greater than what they can buy with their limited amount of money, so prices will begin to fall until equilibrium is achieved. Once again the theory says that the price of goods will be 50% of what they were before. This is a simple example of monetary deflation.

The money in the jar therefore determines the prices of all the goods and services bought and sold in the economy. The examples just given depict what happens, in an extreme case, when the money supply goes up or down. Generally speaking, in the real world, the money supply will change by only a small amount, and consequently the prices will change slowly.

Now, to confuse you, if the money supply goes up, it usually causes inflation. Inflation means that the prices we pay for goods or services are going up. It also means that the value of your money is going down. In the example I gave, where the money supply doubled, it took twice the amount of money to buy, as an example, the same loaf of bread as it did before the money supply doubled. If the loaf of bread cost $1 yesterday, it would cost $2 today. That means your money is now worth only half as much because $1 today would buy only half a loaf of bread. Most people get confused when you tell them their money is losing value as prices go up due to inflation. Of course this means that if the money supply goes down, which is deflation, then, your money becomes more valuable. In the case where money loses half its value (50%), the loaf of bread you bought for $1 yesterday would only costs $0.50 today under conditions of deflation. In other words $1 will now buy you two loaves of bread today instead of just one. Your money is worth twice as much because you can buy twice as much bread with your money today as you could yesterday. Again, it can be confusing to say that when prices drop due to deflation, your money becomes more valuable.

When viewed in this manner, the jar becomes an almost perfect example of what happens when the money supply is increased or decreased and also an almost perfect example of what inflation and deflation are and how they can be caused by changes in the money supply. Inflation and deflation can have many causes, such as temporary shortages, technological changes, or even fear, but the only long-range change in inflation and deflation is caused by changes in the money supply. Usually if prices go up for a reason other than monetary inflation, it means that the producer of those goods or services is making higher profits. If profits are high, there is a sudden interest on the part of potential competitors, who will find creative ways to meet the demand for those goods or services that will bring those competitors healthy profits in the short run, at the same time bringing the supply back in line with demand, and consequently bring the price back down. On the other hand, if supply is too great, prices will fall and companies will cut back on production until supply and demand again come into equilibrium, bringing the price back down. But if the supply of money changes, the markets will change prices in order to achieve equilibrium in supply and demand.

This brings us to the point where we need to define what a depression and a recession are. First, a recession is when the money supply contracts. It can contract because there is a loss of jobs or because people stop spending their money (velocity). It can also happen if a lot of loans (debt) go bad and the banks suddenly have to write off some of their assets. If a bank writes a debt off completely, it removes the same amount of money from the books, which is to say that some of the 90%, on the books only, money in the jar disappears. Some of the money created out of thin air has suddenly disappeared into thin air, just as it was created. Usually, when it's clear that the country has slipped into a recession, the government and the Federal Reserve Board start easing *fiscal and monetary policy,* which increases the amount of money in the economy and thus stimulates the economy. Of course the economy is dynamic and will respond in its own way and time, but the right fiscal and monetary policies can usually right the economy.

Fiscal policy deals with how the government collects and spends money, usually taxes and government programs and entitlements, respectively. By decreasing taxes and increasing spending on government programs, the government can stimulate the economy because it puts more money in the hands of consumers. The usual side effect is that the government builds more debt, but the extra money does tend to stimulate the economy.

Monetary policy has to do with the availability or unavailability of money and the cost of borrowing money. If the banks don't make loans or the interest rate is too high, money slows down (velocity) in the economy. Monetary policy (increasing or decreasing the amount of money in the economy) can increase or decrease the price of money. The price of money, or the price you pay for borrowing money, or for its use, is called interest. By increasing the interest rates, fewer people can afford to borrow money, so the money supply and velocity go down, which causes the economy to contract. On the other hand, if interest rates drop, more people borrow money, and of course if you have money you tend to spend it, and the money supply either goes up or velocity goes up, which tends to stimulate the economy.

We are pretty heavy into the dismal science of economics at this point. I hope it is becoming apparent that if you know nothing about how the banks' function, the dismal science can become even more dismal. If you have read to this point, I hope you do understand more about how banks work and enough about monetary and fiscal policy to have an inkling of what is going on in the real world. I hope it might also be clear that a study of economics should start with banking, and a study of banking should start with a study of the multiplier effect of money.

Now we will look at another extreme: a depression. Once again we have the jar with the money supply. Suppose that something happens to the economy, and all the loans go south. The end result would be that all the money that was created out of thin air would suddenly disappear. This would leave us with nothing but the cash in the bottom of the jar. If this represents the sum total of all the money in the economy, then the price of everything, including labor, would have to be revalued until everything could be bought and sold with only the cash in the bottom of the jar. It would be a huge devaluation (deflation). Prices in theory should drop by about 90% on all goods, services, and labor. This is the extreme example of what a depression is. In reality a depression is when the money supply takes off for the bottom of the jar, and there seems to be nothing between where we are now and the bottom to stop the slide. The money doesn't disappear all at once; it just keeps on disappearing. The slide to the bottom continues, and eventually the slide will stop and equilibrium will be established, but there will be so little money left in the economy that everything will be seriously devalued permanently. A recession is only temporary and a slight decrease in the amount of money in the system (relatively speaking). A depression takes the money supply way down, and it doesn't come back up (at least not in the short run). I will go over this in a little more detail later in the chapter.

If you can't see where this is going, hang in there because it is now time to actually look at who the winners and the losers are when the money supply in the jar changes. Again they may be extreme scenarios, but they reveal plainly what is going on.

Increasing the money supply by around 2% per year to keep the economy stimulated and growing is generally considered inflationary, though only very slightly. If the economy is continually led by increasing the money supply at a more or less constant rate, the economy might experience an inflation rate of 1–2% per year. Economists view this as the cost of making the economy grow and therefore acceptable. Inflation, we learned earlier, causes money to lose its value. It also causes anything denominated in money to lose value. If you hold on to cash in inflationary times, your cash loses purchasing power every day you hold it. This is also true of financial instruments that are denominated in money. When a bank makes a loan today for $1,000.00, it will be repaid with exactly $1,000.00 in the future, sometime after the value of the money has gone down. Holding a loan you have made will cause you to lose money over time under inflationary conditions. In this case the bank will guess at the inflation rate and increase the interest rate on the loans it makes to compensate for the loss of value due to inflation. If the bank wanted to make 7% in interest on its money, and the rate of inflation were 2%, the bank would need to raise the interest rate by 2%, making the total interest 9% in order to cover its losses due to inflation. Again money or anything denominated in money will lose value and create losers. This is true for fixed pensions and annuities. If you retire on a fixed income during inflationary times, that fixed income will lose purchasing power over time and may end up impoverishing you. This is why Social Security payments usually have a cost of living increase during inflationary times. The cost of living increase is supposed to keep up with inflation so the monthly payments don't lose their purchasing power.

During times of inflation, assets that you own go up in value with inflation and do not lose their value. If you pay cash for an asset and keep it, when you go to sell it, the asset will bring a higher price, which will have kept up with the amount of inflation experienced over the same amount of time. Buying assets and paying cash for them is basically a neutral position wherein the buyer neither wins nor loses. Borrowing money at a fixed rate and paying it back over a long period of time can also create winners during times of inflation. If you were to buy a home at a fixed rate of interest and make payments for thirty years, you would find your house payment going down with time under inflationary conditions. If your monthly payment were $500.00 a month and your income was $10,000.00 per year when you bought the home, and thirty years later your salary had gone up with inflation by 100%, you would now be making $20,000.00 per year, and your house payment would still be only $500.00 per month. In effect you are now paying only half as much out of your income for your loan as when you started. The house should have also gone up in value by the same percentage amount as your salary and would be worth, in terms of money, twice as much at the end of the thirty years. This is a good deal for the homeowner. So the winners in inflationary times, when the money supply is expanding, are those who borrow money at fixed rates for long periods of time. The losers are those who hold cash or financial instruments or retirement incomes that have a constant payout for long periods of time.

During times of deflation, the cycle reverses itself. If the deflation is only temporary, the effects aren't so bad, but if deflation continues for a long time, you lose money by borrowing money at a fixed rate. If you owned a home and were paying $500.00 a month in payments while your income was $10,000.00 per year and money were deflating (the money supply was shrinking) over thirty years, if your income were to deflate by 50%, you would be making $5,000.00 and still paying $500.00 a month in house payments. Over the course of a year, you would pay

$6,000.00 in payments, which is more than you would earn in income during the same year.

If you were to make a loan to someone else, you would be on the receiving end of the deal. You would receive a fixed amount of money every period while your money went up in purchasing power. This is also true of pensioners. If you were on a fixed pension, you would get the same amount of money each month as your purchasing power went up.

Since assets go up or down in value in the same proportion as inflation or deflation, if you pay cash for assets, your position is basically neutral, and you are neither a winner nor a loser. Under deflation, losers are the individuals who have borrowed money, and the winners are the people on fixed incomes, or who have loaned out money and receive a fixed payment every period.

Having looked at winners and losers, I would like to revisit the idea of a depression. As money in the economy disappears, everything must be devalued so that those items can be bought with what money is left in the system. This includes labor. As people lose their jobs and can't find jobs that pay as much as their old jobs, they end up taking jobs that pay less. Now they can't make the payments on their home mortgages, their car loans, or even their credit cards. They end up defaulting on their debts and lose their credit ratings. Remember that the dollar amount of the loans doesn't go down as the value of the dollar goes up (deflation). The bank, meanwhile, takes possession of the home. However, it can't sell the house for the amount of the loan, and if the bank can sell the house at all, it must do so at a loss and write down its assets by the amount of the loss. Soon the bank has no equity left and owes everything to depositors and creditors. The bank shuts its doors, which means there are more people out of work and even less money in the system. It is a vicious cycle that continues until equilibrium is finally achieved. The whole process of contraction will take place over time and seems agonizingly strung out. Once again those who have the most to lose during deflationary times are those in debt, those who owe money.

I remember an old-timer telling me about the state of Colorado in 1933. The city of Denver had an unemployment rate of 50%. Every other eligible male worker was out of work. In those days it was mostly the men who worked in the market-place. Outside of Denver, the rest of Colorado had only 33% of eligible male workers out of work. Those figures are a lot worse than the 9–10% unemployment America has experienced since 2008. In 2008 the Federal Reserve Board and the government stepped in to the financial crisis and made sure that we didn't end up in a depression at the time. Since that time the economy has perked back up a little but seems to be rather flat. The Federal Reserve Board has been pumping money into the economy, but it helps only very slightly. As long as the price of assets remains low, the banks remain in limbo, and the economy loses its resil-ience. We have averted a depression but failed to solve many of the underlying problems. I will explain more about why pump-ing money into the banks isn't helping overcome the underlying problems in a later chapter.

Once again there are winners and losers in times of inflation and deflation. Understanding why we become winners and los-ers is important so we can make decisions about our finances.

PART 3

*We have looked at the multiplier effect of money and banks
and how banks use the multiplier effect to their advantage.
We have looked briefly at the Federal Reserve Bank system
and what happens when the money supply expands or contracts.
It is now time to look at some macroeconomic issues
that are related to banks, money and the multiplier effect
that also have an effect on our lives.*

Time has an interesting effect on a number of things.
Living for today compared with living with the long term in mind
can expose one to a whole different set of challenges.
In some ways living for today is just another way of living on the edge.

*** *

In the world of physics, time is considered the fourth dimension
and is believed to be expanding.
In economics it is understood that money can also be expanded.
If time and money can be expanded, then is it not plausible that time
can also be leveraged?

SHORT-TERM VS. LONG-TERM

"Our money supply is based on debt." If this is a reasonable assumption, then you can appropriately ask, "What kind of debt is it based on?" Debt can be a banker's worst nightmare, as well as the proverbial "golden goose." Bankers in the past wanted the debts they took on to be as secure as possible, so they usually sought to ensure that loans were backed by some kind of asset that had value. Homes are built and mortgaged, cars are bought and locked down by a lien, and business loans are usually backed by the assets of the company. Most of these assets have reasonably long life spans that can be measured in years or decades. A house may have a life span of thirty to fifty years or more, a car ten years or more, and most appliances have life spans in excess of five years.

It does wonderful things to the heart and mind when we create something that has lasting value. Creating things that have lasting value or are useful and will provide value for an extended period of time engenders pride in one's work, as well as ongoing value. The real value of a car or a home appears once the lien or mortgage is paid off and before the upkeep becomes greater than the cost of replacing it. It is the object's residual value after it is paid for that gives an asset its real value. There are few things more frustrating than to have something break just as the warranty expires or as you are making the final payment. You usually feel cheated.

Long-term debts ensure that our currency is founded on an underlying base that has a fixed position and security for years to come, whereas short-term debts can mean that the debt underlying our currency can change quickly, leaving our currency in the throes of volatility.

It has been said that the economy of our nation has moved from a manufacturing economy to a service economy. There have been many changes in our economy because of the shift from manufacturing to service. At this point it is said that our economy is moving on into the information economy, and there are even more changes within the economy as we now move to a digital economy composed mainly of digital transfers of information. In looking at these economic trends, it is clear that we have seen a decrease in the manufacture of long-term assets within our country. In all fairness we still produce a lot of long-term assets, just not as many as we used to on a proportional basis.

As we move ever closer to an economy that produces nothing of long-term value, we should expect the money supply, our currency, to become more volatile.

Next I would like to look at what we spend money on in the economy and whether they would be financed by long-term debt or short-term debt. Below is a box with four quadrants made of two rows and two columns. The two columns are long- and short-term debt. The two rows are labeled as necessary and non-necessary. Necessary items would be those things we really need in order to maintain a decent economy or livelihood. Most of us would agree the unnecessary things we could live without, at least in the short run, if we had to, or if necessity were to force us to, to simply do without them.

Value Delivered

	Long Term	Short Term
Unnecessary	Gov Bonds Corp Bonds Corp Stock	Drugs (illegal) Toys Entertainment
Necessary	Office Buildings Mfg Plants Power Plants Ships & Planes Vehicles Mfg & Farm Equip Appliances	Food Clothing Medicine Utilities Services

Customer Needs

Figure #20

When you use things like food, medicine, illegal drugs, utilities, the services or labor of professionals and repairmen, or clothes, the products that make up these goods, assets, or services are here today and gone tomorrow. They don't produce any income for us, relatively speaking. They are normally paid for in cash or through short-term loans and are either necessary or non-necessary. They have no lasting presence, though their value may be great. If you pour money into long-term things like government programs or wars, your money is here and gone, used up with little or nothing left to show for your efforts. The money is used to pay for labor, operating costs, expendable materials and utilities, and the money is immediately gone, often leaving nothing behind of any productive value. These items are labeled long-term because many or all of them are financed through long-term debt when governments simply can't pay for all of the expenses up front.

There are also the necessary long-term items that the economy needs to function: things like housing, manufacturing plants, power stations, office buildings, cars, trucks, farm or manufacturing equipment, and ships. They have relatively long life spans and can be used for security to back loans. They have lasting value.

Let's look at debt for a moment. There is long-term debt that is secured, buildings of all kinds, manufacturing and farm equipment, vehicles, ships, planes, and land, to name some. There is also long-term debt that is unsecured, such as corporate and government bonds, whether federal, state, or local. Government bonds are often used for the purpose of building buildings or major construction projects involving infrastructure. The city in which I live uses bonds to fund landfills and water treatment and sewage processing plants. These operations produce an income from residents that need and pay for these services. The income is used to pay the operational cost and repay the bonds. Many bonds are also used for labor and materials expended on public or civic programs or regulatory activities, or even such things as the collection of taxes. Since these kinds of activities don't produce an income for the government, there is simply no way to secure these bonds to anything other than the government's ability to collect taxes. Corporate bonds are sometimes unsecured because the large corporations are considered too big to be at risk of failure, and the corporations need the money from the sale of bonds for a variety of projects that often make the bonds hard to secure.

Then you have short-term credit, most of which is also unsecured. Purchases by manufacturers and businesses of parts, supplies, or office necessities are some of the possible uses of short-term debt. These are also items that are used up fairly quickly, such as the cost of operating company vehicles, and are thus unsecured. Another area is that of consumer credit. Credit cards are used for almost everything imaginable. Most of the purchases are for items that have short-term to mid-term life expectancies; some could be considered necessary and others unnecessary, but these purchases are unsecured.

As we have moved from a manufacturing economy toward the service and information economy, we have stopped producing items that are considered long-term in nature, or in some cases we have stopped using existing long-term assets, such as plants and manufacturing equipment that remain idle. The implication is that as we move away from the manufacturing economy, we are moving away from creating long-term assets to which we can attach debt and our money supply. If our money supply is based on debt and long-term debt shrinks, then we must move the debt from longer-term assets to shorter-term assets if we wish to maintain the money supply at its current level. If long-term debt decreases and we don't increase our short-term debt holdings, the amount of money taken out in loans will decrease and cause the money supply to shrink, thus deflating the money supply. Generally when debt moves from long-term assets to short-term consumption, these debts also move from being secured to being unsecured. I suppose the debt accumulated on short-term consumption would most likely be credit card debt or short-term business expenses. Because the debt that our money supply is based on is short-term and not anchored to long-term assets, the economy becomes much more fragile. Try imagining an economy and money supply based entirely on credit card debt—definitely an extreme case. Money would turn over very quickly and be completely unsecured. Imagine the financial crisis of 2008 in such a situation. If everyone were to suddenly stop purchasing anything but the absolute necessities, the economy would go through a huge slowdown, money would start disappearing, and you would have the beginnings of a depression. With nothing but unsecured credit card debt, the economic slowdown and shrinkage of the money supply could happen within a few days or weeks and would be devastating. Of course this is an extreme example and doesn't represent reality, but it does serve to demonstrate what happens when an economy and its money supply move from a long-term secured debt base to a short-term unsecured debt base

There are two implications that I need to point out at this point. One is long-term unsecured debts like corporate and government bonds. These can add stability to an economy and money supply but only as long as the corporations and governments remain fiscally stable (able to pay their bills plus payments on the debt). Because the bonds are unsecured, banks and private investors are at risk of losing 100% of their investments. The best example of this is what has been happening in Europe. If Greece or another country were to default on its bonds, it could very well be a 100% write-off. The second is that as manufacturing flees a country, one of the few long-term loan markets that remain is housing and commercial property. If the housing market goes south, the economy and money supply will be seriously endangered. This is perhaps one of the reasons the bursting of the housing bubble has had such a lasting effect on the US economy since 2007.

Short-term debt is perhaps more dynamic and has greater velocity, but it is usually unsecured. Long-term debt that is secured is the bedrock of financial security, at least when we are dealing with the multiplier effect. Long-term unsecured debt can act as an anchor as long as it is not misused by banks or the entities issuing them.

Short-term debt, because of its velocity due to the purchase of short-term goods, may serve to increase leverage in good times, but in bad times the velocity can disappear very fast, either because of a slowdown in purchases or because people walk away from their unsecured debt. The length of term on debt seems to have a leveraging mechanism all its own, which reacts with its own inherent velocity in both good and bad times.

Many economists recommend consumer consumption as a means of spending our way out of recession and the financial crisis our country faces. Our country's weak economy is viewed as a result of consumers cutting back on spending, and if we can only get them to spend more, it will create more jobs and increase production. Of course consumer spending is to a great extent used to buy necessary items that have short-term value. The one major problem with this approach is that so much of past consumption was fueled by consumer credit due to the fact that consumers have no savings. Under such circumstances the only way the population in general can increase its consumption is to do so with more consumer debt. Savings are income that is set aside, and if consumers take money out of savings and use it to buy goods, the economy will definitely perk up, but debt is not income, and using debt as a means of expanding an economy that is already heavily in debt may only exacerbate the problems. This begs the question of whether unsecured short-term debt is the real solution to spending our way out of our financial problems. If you understand the relationship between secured and unsecured debt as well as the longevity of the debt, the assumption appears to be questionable. It might be interesting to note here that China has done fairly well during the great recession. It is pointed out that its huge exports have helped sustain it. The other major factor that is pointed to for its success is its command economy. It is claimed that the state seems better placed to control an economy than the free market. One of the most important things about China's ability to deal with the great recession has been its savings. Its culture encourages savings among its citizens and the government itself had huge monetary reserves. When they needed the money to sustain their economy they had it without resorting to increased indebtedness.

In conclusion I hope it is insightful that long-term secured debt, as opposed to short-term unsecured debt, has a stabilizing effect upon our currency and consequently upon our economy and can reduce the volatility of our economy.

The edge could be the cutting edge of a blade
or just the beginning of the precipice,
but walking the edge can be either an adrenaline rush
from the pinnacle of accomplishment and adulation
or it can be the harbinger of pain and disaster.

LIVING ON THE EDGE

When I was a kid, the old folks used to talk about saving for a rainy day. Bad things happen to good people as well as the bad, and, like the weather, rainy days aren't always predictable. So saving for a rainy day was looked upon as having merit.

When I went to college, I had to take production classes as a part of the general business curriculum. Inventories were a big part of understanding production. Inventory had to do with raw materials or parts used in production as well as the finished product on hand. The ideal amount of inventory to have on hand for production was what the business needed to maintain production in order to supply its customers under the toughest or most unusual circumstances. The amount of finished inventory needed was what you would need to meet a sudden increase in sales or normal sales if something happened to slow down production. Machines break down, people get sick, supplies are slow showing up, or utilities go out due to a storm. So many things can go wrong that you keep a little extra on hand. Sometimes inventory was increased during the slow season and allowed to fall during the busy season so that the business could maintain a steady production and avoid layoffs. The yearly business cycle was an important item to track. Inventory was what you fell back on when there were problems or in order to maintain steady employment. Unions became a very real problem if production wasn't steady, so businesses liked to keep production steady. Back then people believed in Murphy's Law and tried to account for it.

In some areas, local governments tax inventories, and sometimes there are good reasons to tax inventories, but in other cases small inventories are a simple matter of common sense and planning. However, if inventories are taxed, a business wants to have as little inventory sitting around as possible. Capitalism is about maximizing profits through increasing sales and minimizing expenses and also about how you achieve those goals, which includes inventories and production, among other activities.

About the time I graduated from college, computers were taking hold as a business tool. Over the years the ability of the computer to crunch numbers and create models has supplied businesses with the ability to cut inventories to the quick and predict when to increase or decrease production on a near-daily basis. Cutting inventory to the quick makes your current bottom line look better than it did in the last reporting period because you are decreasing an expense and turning materials over faster. But with every new reporting period, it gets harder to cut more from inventory, and you eventually can't squeeze any more expenses out of the equation through inventory reduction. Controlling inventories closely also shows where there is excess production capacity, so production capacity, which includes downtime and maintenance and production capabilities, is also cut to the quick. Living on the cutting edges is what it is all about, and computers have given us the precision to do it. Good managers know how to cut it close, but great managers can cut things to the quick and ride the razor's edge.

In 2011 Murphy's Law struck in the form of an earthquake and tsunami in northeast Japan, destroying production facilities that sold parts to companies all over the world. Most of the companies they supplied had only one supplier. Of course those manufacturers who needed the parts from northern Japan didn't keep large inventories of the parts they needed on hand. In the past those parts had been available by next-day air if the company was desperate. The tsunami shot holes in the idea that you don't need to keep your own inventories for that rainy day that never seems to come. Most businesses that depended on supplies from northeast Japan were left twiddling their thumbs until they could find new suppliers or their regular suppliers came back online.

Citizens of the United States and perhaps most of Western civilization have come to lean on credit. It seems rational to believe you can push to the limit and live on the edge when it comes to credit. A lot of people do it, and you seldom see or hear individual stories about neighbors going over the edge; most people don't like to talk about being in those situations. In financial matters today, credit is a safety net you keep in place for when it looks like you are about go over the edge. Forget saving for a rainy day; if things get tight, we can break out the credit card or run to the bank for a loan, and it will tide us over until things improve. Using credit is so easy, especially when interest rates are so low. In counterpoint, savings happen to be spare income that you have set aside. Debt, while handy, is a drain on your future income. If a business or an individual has lots of debt and something goes wrong and income is lost, even for a short time, he, she, or it will find themselves in a real bind. The other scenario is what happens when you reach your credit limit. Suddenly you have no cushion to fall back on.

Banks also know how to push the limits and walk on the edge. The great juggling act is both a challenge and a rush. Banks get leveraged out so far that the profits are huge and salaries and bonuses go up, as well as the parties and lifestyles. But if you go over the edge, the fall is not only down, it is also leveraged. By finding new financial vehicles where banks have no regulation, as in the banks don't have to report those financial vehicles and no one knows where the banks' risks are, or as in the financial vehicles are so new that regulation doesn't exist yet, the bank can "walk the edge." The banks did this in the years leading up to the financial crisis of 2008. Then something happened that no one saw coming. Overnight loans are unsecured and all-important to the banking industry, and with the default of one major bank and its spill over into other major banks, all of a sudden every bank was at risk, and no bank had a way of knowing what any other bank's potential risk was. Every banker realized he could not count on any other bank to pay back its unsecured overnight loans. Overnight loans disappeared and the banking system came to a very quick halt. Then the central banks stepped in and provided all the money to bail out the banks, which is what they are supposed to do in a crisis.

Some people and businesses don't have anyone behind them to bail them out when things turn for the worse. For individuals and businesses living on the edge, the financial crisis of 2008 was a disaster. For the individuals and businesses that were prepared, or not living on the edge, it has only been an ongoing pain or a problem that has at least some solution. In this day and age, we have learned to live on the edge in so many ways, and it just seems to be the way the world works at the moment. But there is also comfort and a sense of well-being that comes from saving for a rainy day or having the capacity to carry on normally when things go wrong. Savings and inventories carry a certain amount of financial burden due to lost earnings or profits, but if you can live with the present lost opportunities, you can avoid disaster during a crisis. Living on the edge can be exhilarating and even profitable, but it can also be painful because there are risks associated with those behaviors.

Then there are governments. I suppose how you feel about a government depends on whether you think governments are really just an agent or extension of the people (democratic), an independent agent capable of looking out for its own interests in a disinterested fashion that has nothing to do with the people (meritocracy of various forms), or just an extension of the individuals who run the government for their own purposes (autocratic). Regardless of how you choose to look at government, most Western governments seem to have overextended themselves financially. The US government has done a number of things in the realm of finance that are pretty crazy. One of the biggest of these is probably that it makes the rules or laws and sometimes exempts itself from those laws. There are two methods of accounting: accrual and cash. Every business in the country must report insurance and pensions and future liabilities using the accrual method on its balance sheet, which shows how much the company will eventually have to pay out when the pensions and insurance come due. It is a way of looking at risk and forcing insurance companies and pension plans and banks to assess their future risks today. Unfortunately the US government doesn't have to do what it requires everyone else to do. It gets to account for everything using the cash method, so the future pay-outs don't show on its balance sheets. If our government had to use the accrual method, our national debt would look more like $140 trillion rather than its current $14 trillion. The $140 trillion is probably a gross exaggeration, but if the government had to list its future potential payouts for pensions, military insurance, and Social Security payments to civil servants and citizens, our nation's indebtedness would be huge; $14 trillion would be a gross understatement.

I remember back in the 1980s when Congress was looking for easy money and decided to borrow all the money from the Social Security funds. Their justification was "we are borrowing it from ourselves [another government agency], so we don't have to report it as a part of the budget deficit." Unfortunately the new securities issued and placed on the Social Security balance sheet might not show up in the national debt, but they will still have to be repaid someday—and with interest.

No matter how you choose to look at creative financing, most Western governments have been out walking on the edge, thinking the day of accountability would never come. I think it was Warren Buffet who said something to the effect of "everyone looks good when they are out swimming at the beach, but it is only when the tide goes out you discover who has been swimming naked." It seems that recent history has had a way of turning the tide out in many facets of our world. The world of business, personal finance, investments banking, and government has seen the tide go out, and unfortunately too many have been left standing not quite so pretty as they once thought.

The edge is a great place for the thrill seeker, but as a way of life it tends to come up a little short. In spite of it all, the majority of humans seem willing to live with the risks associated with living on the edge in their personal lives, their businesses, and their governments.

Rock climbers sometimes fall.
When the climber gets to the end of his rope, there is a sudden jerk,
and then what?
The answer may depend on whether the rope is attached
to a quality harness or looped around his neck.
It is interesting to note that the majority of rock climbers,
who understand the risks involved, prefer a quality harness, and
the minority, the really hard-core climbers,
prefer no rope at all.

THE END OF CREDIT

Credit card debt is interesting. The available credit on a card is a standing loan to be taken out on demand anytime the bearer of the card wishes. Loans in general are used to increase the money supply and also spur the economy forward. Loans made to businesses can create expansion within businesses and therefore more output and more jobs, which in turn allow more people to buy goods and services. Credit cards, instead of being used to expand businesses directly, are a means of expanding the purchasing power of the consumers. The consumers push up demand for products, and the result is that the businesses sell more products, take out more loans, expand production, hire new people, and grow to support the new demand. Bank loans to businesses can be viewed as a top-down production stimulus to the economy, while credit card loans to customers can be viewed as a bottom-up stimulus to business production. In either scenario, an increase in business loans or an increase in consumer credit, you would expect the economy to be spurred forward with a resulting increase in jobs as well as increased production and sales.

At this point I would like to point out one of the problems associated with credit card debt. Again we will look at credit card debt from an extreme point of view so we can better see the problem. Assume that all credit card holders maxed out their cards and used up all their available credit. At this point consumers no longer have any credit. They now have to buy everything with the money they have in their checking accounts, savings accounts, or whatever is in their wallets and piggy banks. Now suppose the credit card companies suddenly increased everyone's credit limit by 10%. Suddenly everyone would have not only the money in their accounts and wallets but also 10% more in credit. At this point imagine that all the credit card holders again went out and immediately used up the extra 10% on their credit cards. Consumer credit is again maxed out. This new surge of spending would once again stimulate the economy. However, at this point the consumers are back to spending only what is in their accounts or wallets. At the same time, consumers now have a larger payment to make on their new level of credit card debt. If the banks suddenly realized the consumers had truly reached their credit limits, at which point they could no longer afford an increase in their monthly payments, the credit card companies, banks, would be forced to withhold continued increases in the credit card limits. At this point demand for goods would level out to somewhere lower than it was during the time of easy credit, or, in other words, demand would decline by perhaps as much as 10% (obviously a guess), but businesses would need to cut back on production and lay people off. Times aren't looking too good, so consumers determine they need to cut back on their level of debt. Each consumer decides to tighten his belt and cut back by 10% so he or she can cut down on expenses and gain a little breathing room while paying off some credit card debt. Now demand has been reduced another 10%, and again businesses have to cut back on production by yet another 10%. Of course this all causes the economy to shrink substantially.

Credit is not income; it is a liability, and this is just as true of credit card debt as it is of any other form of debt. If everyone is spending more than the amount of their income, say by 10%, when they hit their collective credit limit and find themselves having to purchase on a cash basis, the economy will suddenly find itself running on 10% less purchasing power and will have to cut back by 10%. On top of this, if people wish to cut back and reduce their debts or get out of debt altogether, the economy will shrink still further until people are again willing to spend in accordance with their current incomes or fall back into the trap of the credit-income disease. When people, businesses, or governments spend beyond their current incomes for a sustained period of time, they eventually run the risk of running out of credit. The credit-income disease is real. Credit can be a great stimulus to an economy, particularly from the consumer side; bottom-up demand is great, but when the consumer's credit comes to an end, then what?

I would like to look at credit card debt from a different point of view. This is an extreme view in which we start with no credit card debt and will ignore the fact that there are payments due on the debt once created. With no credit card debt an economy would run on the income of the individuals within the country. The combined incomes of the individuals would be the natural limit determining what would be purchased within the economy. Now let's assume all the individuals were issued a new credit card. During the next year all of those consumers purchased enough items on their credit cards to increase the size of the economy by ten percent in dollar terms. In short we have increased consumer demand by ten percent through the introduction of credit cards. In this case one of two things ought to happen: either prices will inflate so that the amount of production will remain the same or prices will remain the same and production will increase by ten percent. If prices go up we have true monetary inflation with its own set of consequences. This is not the direction I want to go, so we won't go there. On the other hand if production expands by ten percent, we can assume, if we over simplify, that labor and business will also expand by ten percent. Now, in order for business to maintain this new level of production in the coming year, consumers will once again need to spend, in dollar terms, ten percent more money than their collective incomes. In other words credit card debt is being used as current income and unless the ten percent extra is spent every year the economy will have to contract by the same amount. At the same time consumers, in the aggregate, are adding ten percent of the amount of their income to the balances on their credit cards every year.

In this example we have ignored some significant realities, however, if one takes the example to its logical conclusion, the individuals will eventually reach the end of their credit limits and the economy will shrink by the amount of ten percent. This is the end of credit. Some people might prefer to call it the "limits" of credit, but whichever term you wish to use the result will probably be the same.

Of course much of government spending goes to civil servants and military personnel, pensions, and welfare handouts.

Very little is used for long-term production of goods or services, but again it provides jobs and security for individuals as well as a stimulus to the economy. And if governments pay for all or a major part of this stimulus through debt, they will either run out of credit and have to cut back, tax the people more heavily, or start printing money.

Greece has reached the end of its credit. Even with two bail-outs and forcing private investors to take a 50% loss on the Greek government bonds, Greece is so far in debt that it won't ever be able to repay its national debt. On top of this, the Eurozone is forcing Greece to move into austerity, which is shrinking its economy so the government takes in less revenue from taxes.

If Greece defaults on everything, it may take down half the banks in Europe because those banks are holding the major chunk of Greek debt and are already leveraged out eighty to one on their equity.

Unless the Eurozone and the European Central Bank bailout several national governments and the banks within their countries, the Eurozone may be beyond help because it may well have reached the end of its credit or even gone beyond the limit, as the case may be. In all likelihood the European Central bank will probably print enough money to avoid default of their currency.

Of course the banks play their part in all this. They make loans to businesses, hand out credit cards, and buy government debt. In the process they of course make money on the interest, but more so they are creating wealth, of which much will fall to them.

Another interesting point about the end of credit concerns banks and their use of the multiplier effect. Let's assume the same balance sheet from the end of the chapter on equity (Figure #21):

	Assets	Liabilities	
(Cash)	$21,000.00	$210,000.00 (Deposits)	Current Liabilities
Current Assets	————	————	
		$10,000.00 (CD's)	Long Term Liabilities
Long Term Assets (Loans)	$180,000.00 $20,000.00 $9,000.00	$10,000.00	Equity
Totals	$230,000.00	$230,000.00	

Figure #21

The asset to equity ratio is about 4.3%, which is above the allowable limit. Let's assume for a minute that the bank was able to come up with an additional $7,000.00 in new deposits and using the multiplier effect they were able to loan out $6,300.00 (90% of $7,000.00) that would eventually create a total of $63,000.00 in loans and deposits. This would leave deposits at $210,000.00 + $7,000.00 + $63,000.00 = $280,000.00 with $7,000.00 + $21,000.00 = $28,000.00 in cash which would bring the totals at the bottom to $300,000.00 for both columns (see figure #22). This would put the equity to asset ratio at just above 3%, which meets its regulatory requirement. If a bank finds itself in this position during severe economic times when property values have decreased by 25% and most other assets are on the verge of being devalued, what can the Federal Reserve do to help the bank? Looking at the balance sheet, the Federal

Reserve could make deposits at the bank. This would increase the available cash in the bank, which in turn would increase the total assets. If total assets went up but equity remained the same, the bank would end up below the 3% equity to capital ratio. If the Federal Reserve were to make loans to the bank, the same thing would happen: cash and total assets would go up, but equity would remain the same. Unfortunately the bank would find itself, once again, in the same position; if it borrowed more money or attracted more depositors, its total assets would go up, while equity would not.

This leaves assets and equity that the Federal Reserve and the bank can deal with. If the Federal Reserve were to buy assets from the bank at full price, cash would go up but total assets would remain the same. That brings us to the conclusion that the only thing the bank can do is raise its equity position. This means the bank must sell more stock or make a lot more in profits.

If the Federal Reserve were to buy stock in the bank, depending on the type of stock, the Federal Reserve would end up owning part of the bank or having a vested interest in the bank, which at best creates moral hazard and at worst something that is akin to nationalization of the bank. Getting involved in the equity of banks just doesn't look right or appeal to a responsible regulator. This narrows the range of options down to about one; selling more stock to the public. If the stock market is also down, it is not a favorable time to sell stock. If the banks are struggling, maybe no one will want to purchase stock anyway. As the bank increases the amount of stock issued, it means profits that would go to dividends would be divided into smaller chunks, and if dividend rates begin to fall, it tends to make the price of stock go down, which can further hinder the sale of stock and the acquisition of new capital (equity).

One new idea is to allow the banks investors to take a loss for their bad choice of investment in the bank. By issuing debt, bonds, that is convertible into equity the banks debt can now be converted into equity and subject to loss. Debt or bonds usually get paid before all else so the banks creditors suffer no loss if the bank goes under. But this is not so if the bonds are convertible to equity.

Looking at to the balance sheet we just created, let's look at another problem (figure #22).

	Assets		Liabilities	
	(Cash) $28,000.00		$280,000.00 (Deposits)	Current Liabilities
Current Assets	————		————	
			$10,000.00 (CD's)	Long Term Liabilities
Long Term Assets (Loans)	$63,000.00 $180,000.00 $20,000.00 $9,000.00		$10,000.00	Equity
Totals	$300,000.00		$300,000.00	

Figure #22

	Assets	Liabilities	
	Assets	**Liabilities**	
(Cash)	$33,000.00	$280,000.00 (Deposits)	**Current Liabilities**
Current Assets	————	————	
		$10,000.00 (CD's)	**Long Term Liabilities**
Long Term Assets (Loans)	$63,000.00 $180,000.00 $20,000.00 $9,000.00	$15,000.00	**Equity**
Totals	$305,000.00	$305,000.00	

Figure #23

Assume the bank increased its equity by 50% through any means possible. The bank would now have $15,000.00 in equity (Figure #23). If the bank had to sell part or all of its loans for a loss that equaled just 2% of total assets, or $6,000.00, it would now have equity of only $9,000.00 (Figure #24) because it would have to write its equity side of the balance sheet down by the same amount as the asset side, which would put the bank under its 3% ratio limit by a mere fraction (299,000 / 9 = 33.2, which is less than the 1 to 33.333 required by a little under 00.1). By selling $180,000.00 loan for $6,000.00 less than their original value and adding the cash from the sale to the balance sheet as cash we end up with $207,000.00 in cash (Figure #24).

	Assets	Liabilities	
Current Assets	(Cash) $207,000.00 ———	$280,000.00 (Deposits) ———	Current Liabilities
		$10,000.00 (CD's)	Long Term Liabilities
Long Term Assets (Loans)	$63,000.00 $20,000.00 $9,000.00	$9,000.00	Equity
Totals	$299,000.00	$299,000.00	

Figure #24

Going back to the balance sheet earlier in this chapter, we would have figure #22. If the bank were to double its equity (figure #25) it would still have the ability
to write down its assets by only about 4% overall. If the
bank were to write down assets by $11,000.00 ($11,000.00
is 3.7% of $310,000.00) after doubling its equity, its
balance sheet would look exactly like the one in figure #24 ($310,000.00 – $11,000.00 = $299,000.00).
Doubling the bank's equity would be a massive undertaking
and would probably never happen, and the bank would still
be able to write its assets down by only about 4%.

By going out into the market and selling as much stock as
already exists, doubling the amount of stock, the bank cuts the
ownership of the original stockholders in half. Many companies do
split their stock two for one, which doubles the amount of stock.

	Assets	Liabilities	
Current Assets	(Cash) $38,000.00 ———	$280,000.00 (Deposits) ———	Current Liabilities
		$10,000.00 (CD's)	Long Term Liabilities
Long Term Assets (Loans)	$63,000.00 $180,000.00 $20,000.00 $9,000.00	$20,000.00	Equity
Totals	$310,000.00	$310,000.00	

Figure #25

However, each stockholder ends up with twice as many shares, so each stockholder still owns the same percentage of the company or the same percentage of the company's assets and receives the same dollar amount of dividends as before, but selling more stock only waters down ownership and dividends.

If the assets in an economy are deflating or are already deflated, the bank either cannot make loans because it has reached the end of its ability to add assets to its balance sheet or is so at risk that it needs to keep all the cash it can and refuses to take on the increased risk of more loans while reverse leverage ominously stares it in the face. The more cash the bank holds, the better the bank's position, because cash is an asset that is not written down, though holding cash doesn't generate any profits or lower its equity to assets ratio either. At the same time, if the economy is bad and asset prices are way down, if the people and businesses who took out the loans are still making payments, the bank doesn't have to write its assets down immediately, though it may eventually have to write them down. However, the bank understands the risk that it faces, for if things turn worse it will undoubtedly see some loans fail, the bank will have to write down those assets, and it could eat up its equity. Given those circumstances banks are hesitant to make new loans and afraid to give up cash. In effect the bank has reached the end of its credit.

When times are tough and asset prices are way down, there is really very little that can be done to help the situation. The one solution is that the value of assets must come up to its original level or higher, which will give the banks room to maneuver. Of course there are two ways to bring the price of assets up. One is to get the economy growing and let supply and demand bring the prices back up. The other is to create monetary inflation that will bring the price of assets up, but inflation creates its own winners and losers.

Of course we have been looking at the extreme here. The real question is, in reality, is there really such a thing as the end of credit? For the individual, a business or perhaps for the individual bank, the answer seems to be an obvious yes, but can it also be true for an entire industry, such as banks, or a huge economy, the entire population, or even all nations? Maybe the jury is still out, or maybe, in the end, you will have to be the judge.

For those who are risk takers,
there is usually something to be gained from the risk:
the pie in the sky, the pot of gold at the end of the rainbow,
fame, or power. The greater the risk, the greater
the reward, and of course
the risk always seems worth it.

BONDS AND SWAPS

I have read a lot of things about mortgage bonds and sometimes it is hard to determine what is truth and what is fiction. To start with a bond is a loan. Interest is generally paid yearly or quarterly but none of the principle of the loan is repaid until the bond comes due and is then paid in a lump sum.

The bank can do a number of things with a mortgage once a mortgage is created. It can keep the loan or it can sell the loan. It can put the mortgage in a portfolio with other mortgages and sell them as a package. The buyer has to buy all of them or none. The buyer can't pick and choose which loans he will buy, this allows the bank to get rid of less desirable loans along with its better ones. The buyer of course would have access to all the information on all of the mortgages and would make an offer on the package as a whole. Once the investor has purchased the portfolio he can unbundle it and do as he pleased with each loan. In either type of sale the bank no longer has an interest in the mortgage or mortgages because the buyer now owns them. The sale of the portfolio was not a bond, loan, but a sale.

After a mortgage is created it can also be bundled with other mortgages and sold as a marketable security, this is called securitization. There are three things that come into consideration when this happens: who owns the mortgages, who manages the mortgages (collects the payments and deposits them, pays the insurance and taxes on the properties associated with the mortgages and collects delinquencies) and the loan which is given in exchange for the bond. These three things can be held by two or more entities. The bank can own and manage the mortgages for the bond holder or the bank can manage them while the bond holder owns the mortgages and holds the bond. Most bond holders don't want to manage the loans, it is a simple investment of money, and they are therefore less likely to own the bonds. There can also be a third party who manages the mortgages and pays the bondholder while the bank owns the mortgages. Or a third party could negotiate the deal, buying the mortgages and selling the bond and doing the management. There are many possibilities and it is all legal as long as the transaction is transparent and open and no fraudulent misrepresentations are made. Because the mortgages are securitized the bond can be bought and sold much like stock, but the mortgages have to remain bundled together.

In the lead up to the financial crisis of 2008 there were a lot of mistakes made in the creation of mortgages. There were mistakes made by investors as they believed risks had been ameliorated. There were mistakes made by credit agencies and regulators too. It all came together quite unexpectedly with rather dramatic results.

At this point I would like to take you through an example of the creation and sale of a mortgage bond. It is way simplified but the things that are presented and some of the problems that arise from it are all interrelated in whichever scenario you pick for the creation of the mortgage bond. They all share many of the same common denominators.

As we have seen earlier, a bank can make a loan on a home. In doing so it creates a mortgage that has an accompanying income stream. The bank can turn around and sell the mortgage as a financial asset and make the rest of the principal, minus the discount, as a profit. The discount is written off as a loss, which is a disincentive to sell the mortgage, but at the same time the bank receives a large chunk of cash for the sale. The only real choice is whether it wants the income stream or whether it wants to take the profit now and reinvest it. But what if the bank can do both at the same time? What if the bank can keep the income stream and cash the mortgage in at the same time? Well, someone along the way figured out how to do it. Once again we will take an example, and it may not be absolutely true to reality, but the principle is.

The bank can take a number of mortgages that it possesses and bundle them together. Say the bank takes ten mortgages and the value of the ten mortgages is $1,000,000.00. It can bundle them together and sell a bond with the mortgages as the basis of the bond. Let's say it sells the bond for $900,000.00 or at a 10% discount. Selling the bond for a little less than the value of the mortgages may seem safer because the mortgages could lose 10% of their value and not leave the bond upside down. By doing this the bank is keeping the income stream from the mortgages and taking the profits now. It also does not have to count the discount as a loss, which it would if the bank sold the mortgages. Bonds are usually unsecured and based on the good faith and credit of the borrower. In the end the bank is saying that they have the mortgages and that they are viable and will pay off in a timely manner, and so the bank will have the money to pay the interest and pay off the bond when it comes due. The bank now has the income stream plus $900,000.00 to loan out, creating more wealth and income.

There is a second way of looking at the bond that was just created. Since a bond is a loan, the investors are loaning their money to the bank, and in return they will get the principal back at the due date on the bond, plus a yearly interest payment. In either scenario the bond will be listed as a liability or a debt on the bank's balance sheet, and the $900,000.00 will be listed as cash on the asset side of the balance sheet. We can look at it either way, but the bottom line is the bank is keeping the income stream from the mortgages and collecting $900,000.00, which it can loan out for its own purposes according to the multiplier rate and make loans of at least $8,000,000.00.

In the example above the bank is retaining ownership of the mortgages and will be the one responsible for the management of the mortgages. The investor making the loan to the bank probably does not want the responsibility of taking care of the mortgages on a month to month basis. What the investor wants is a return on his money while the bank is using it and then to get the principle back when the bond comes due.

When I first heard of mortgage bonds, I thought it sounded a lot like selling the house twice, but of course that is not what is happening. If the bank were to sell the mortgage, it would reap the profits and take a loss on the discount but no longer own the mortgage and the mortgage's income stream. In reality, when the bank sells the bond, it creates a debt on a debt. You have two debts that are underwritten by one or more pieces of property. The property is collateral for the first debt, which is the mortgage, but it is not collateral for the second debt. The income and the future value of that income are underwriting the bond. There is no guarantee as to the future value of the underlying properties and even less of a guarantee as to the income from the mortgages or the income's future value. By creating the bond the risks are compounded

The bottom line seems to be that creating debt on debt increases the risks. If the money borrowed from the sale of the bond is reinvested in mortgages, then the bank should be able, in theory, to create a new bond based on the new mortgages. Now the bank has ten times as many bonds based on the original mortgages, and it is heavily invested in the housing market. By using the multiplier effect of money, the bank will make loans to the tune of ten times the original income from the bond. Even if the prices of the properties were not inflating, the bank would have created a bubble in its loan portfolio. If the housing market suddenly went south, it would be caught with all these mortgages that it couldn't sell because the mortgages were underwriting the bonds. They also couldn't write down the value of the loans because then the bonds would not be fully backed (underwritten). And if one of the mortgages went into default, what would the bank do when the mortgage was part of the underwriting of the bond?

Now for a short story from my daughter, who lives in the Phoenix area. When the housing market in Phoenix went bust, a lot of her neighbors were renting nice homes from investors who had purchased the homes when houses were inflating in price like crazy. The houses lost as much as 50% of their market value very quickly, and they couldn't be sold. Most of the investors walked away from their mortgages because they could no longer make the payments and took a loss on their investments. In some cases the renters had been living in these houses and not paying any rent for over a year. What a deal for the renters! I was flabbergasted! Why didn't the banks foreclose on the properties and start charging rent if they couldn't sell them? Now I suspect that the homes were tied up with bonds and the bank couldn't do anything with the property without writing down the underlying value of the bonds too. The banks were stuck and could do nothing, which meant they couldn't even collect rent on the properties. It was crazy. The banks could also have been invested in credit swaps and couldn't afford to foreclose because it would trigger the payouts on the swaps.

Swaps—where did swaps come from? Well, I guess it is time to talk about credit swaps!

Credit default swaps belong to a class of financial instruments that are called derivatives. The first thing you should understand about a credit default swap is it is an insurance policy. The second thing to understand is it is not called insurance, because if it were called insurance it would be regulated like all other insurance, which it is not. The third thing to understand is that the credit default swap is not created or sold by an insurance company for the same reason it is not called insurance. Most credit default swaps are created by banks, equity funds, or outfits that have a lot of money. Perhaps the last thing you need to know is that credit default swaps are totally opaque. Only the people who issue them and the people who buy them know what the terms are, what they cover, and for how long and how much. No one else really even knows whether they even exist or not. There are absolutely no rules and no regulation. At this point in time, governments are starting to crack down on the swap market in an effort to make it more transparent and make it harder for financial institutions to create them in the first place.

Because swaps are so opaque no one knows much about swaps and it opens the door for all kinds of shady dealings. I have read about situations that border on gambling and racketeering but at this point, precisely because so little is known, I don't even know if they are true. Here I will be treating swaps as if they are being created for legal and beneficial purposes.

Credit default swaps are supposed to spread around the risks from the creation of risky financial instruments. Many subprime mortgages were bundled as bonds and then sold and then had credit default swaps attached to them to ensure that the bond-holders got their money back if or when the bonds (underlying mortgages) went bust. In retrospect about the only thing we really know about credit default swaps is their general purpose and the fact that they do exist and create a climate in which banks and investors believe there is little risk. Unfortunately they can also create a climate of fear—fear because insurance has risk and the outfit that has to pay up when the swap is triggered will take a serious hit, but no one knows how great of a hit or even who will get hit. It is precisely the unknown that creates the fear.

The purpose of a credit default swap is to share risk, spread it around, and thus minimize risk. Let's take an example. Bank X creates a mortgage bond with one hundred mortgages as the basis of the bond. Since mortgages carry risk, owners sometimes default, and the bank wants to cover some of the risk involved if part of the mortgages go into default. If 20% of the mortgages in a bond failed, the bond would be in a position where it could also be at risk of default. In this case Bank X may go to Bank Y and propose that it insure the bond by doing a credit default swap. Of course it would do this at the time of the creation of the bond or shortly after, but before it was obvious that there might be a problem. The details can be whatever the two banks agree to, which includes the payments to Bank Y for the insurance policy, the trigger that makes Bank Y pay the insurance claim, and the time period for which the bond will be covered. Once terms have been agreed upon and a contract signed, Bank X will pay Bank Y so much money, as an insurance premium, probably every quarter, and Bank Y will guarantee that the bondholders will be paid in full if a certain level of default on the underlying mortgages is reached. A certain level of defaults has to be reached, as agreed to by both banks, before Bank Y has to put up the money to cover the bond. By creating the credit default swap, Bank X doesn't have to carry all the risk involved in a default. In this situation Bank X will not want to trigger the credit default swap because as soon as it does it will have to write down the value of the underlying mortgages, which will begin the process of deleveraging on its books. At the same time, Bank X has limited its liability to a loss of 20% of the value of the bonds plus any loss on the defaulted mortgages. If the bond takes over a 20% loss, then Bank Y will pay out all of the money necessary to cover the investors in the bond but doesn't have any responsibility for the actual losses on the mortgages. The payout from Bank Y could be anywhere from 1% to 80% of the value of the bond, depending on the way the swap was written. In other words the two banks have swapped some or all of the potential loss through an insurance policy. As long as Bank X can keep mortgages that are technically in default on its books, it doesn't have to recognize the loss, or in other words write down its assets (deleverage), and doesn't have to trigger the default swap. If Bank Y never has to pay up on the default, it earns the insurance premium as profit without having to pay any money to keep the bond afloat. If Bank Y considered the risk great enough, it could even create a credit default swap with Bank Z so as to limit its liability if it had to pay out on the defaulted bond. The swaps can go on forever from one bank to another if the risks are deemed great enough. The bond holder can also have a swap created to make sure he gets his money back.

Credit default swaps can be created to cover losses on any financial instrument as long as the risk involved in the instrument makes it look reasonable to pay for the insurance. At one point in the Eurozone's negotiations to save the Greek government from defaulting, the negotiators got private investors in Greek bonds to agree to a voluntary write-down of the Greek bonds they held by around 50%; in other words the private investors would automatically take a 50% loss on the bonds today and take an even greater loss if Greece did a total default later on. The reason for getting the private investors to accept a 50% write-down was specifically to avoid triggering the credit default swaps on the bonds. If the investors and the Greek government labeled the write-down as a 50% default, rather than as a voluntary write-down, the credit default swaps would be triggered. By forcing only the private investors to take losses, they also saved other institutions, like governments, the International Monetary Fund, and the central banks, from having to take losses, which would have triggered credit swaps among the European banks, forcing them to cough up on the insurance. This might well have taken down a lot of European banks. No one really knew how deeply involved the banks were in insuring the Greek bonds, but since it might put some banks under, no one wanted to find out just how extensive the credit swaps were.

In 2008 when the mortgage and housing bubble burst and Lehman Brothers went under and AIG had to be bailed out, all of a sudden all the banks realized they had no idea what any other bank was hiding in its books in the way of shaky mortgage bonds and credit default swaps. Lehman Brothers and AIG were heavily invested in mortgage bonds and swaps and their collapse sent ripples throughout the rest of the financial community. All of a sudden mortgage bonds were next to worthless and swaps were being triggered and many banks didn't know if they would remain solvent much less if any other bank would be solvent at the end of the day. Because of the lack of transparency, no bank was willing to give overnight unsecured loans, to other banks. Without the overnight loans, the great juggling act came to a sudden halt. It was described as a loss of liquidity. I hope you will recognize that a loss of liquidity means the bank has no way of covering a shortfall in its 10% reserve requirement and maybe even the bills that were coming in, and if it runs out of cash it is forced to shut its doors. Such was the predicament the banks found themselves in during the early stages of the financial crisis. Of course the Federal Reserve, as well as other central banks, bailed the banks out temporarily, but even then some banks never recovered. But it did save us from a depression. If most of the banks had gone under all at the same time, it would have been cataclysmic, to say the least.

It appears that credit default swaps could be a good thing, particularly if they were open and transparent enough to avoid the creation of fear and paralysis. Unfortunately the only way we may get such openness and transparency will be to regulate the industry so that it has to report and record the credit default swaps for the insurance that they are, thus exposing the swaps as the risks they pose.

The trade deficit is an important issue to you and me
but even more so to our children's children
and foreign powers!

THE TRADE DEFICIT

Back in the old days, way back there, there was a gold standard in which the currency of the various nations was in fact coins minted in gold or sometimes in another precious metal, such as silver. Even in more modern times, many countries have used varying types of a gold standard which has had varying effects on their respective currencies. In the United States, it meant coins had to be made containing a given percentage of precious metals, among other things, or the banks had to back paper money with precious metals stored somewhere in a vault (Fort Knox, for example). But my real interest is not so much in the way our currency is controlled within our country as it is in the part our currency plays in international trade and how that trade affects us.

In more ancient history, business between countries or kingdoms was conducted in terms of gold. Currency of a particular country was usually in the form of gold and silver coins. The precious metals had universal as well as intrinsic value as compared with the paper money we use today. If you wanted to buy spices from traders who had traveled from far countries, you paid for them in coins made of precious metals. Silver was acceptable but didn't have the same value as gold, so you paid more by weight in silver for those spices than you would if you paid in gold.

When a trader sold his goods at his destination he would, being a trader, use the gold to buy something else to take back home and sell for a profit. The trader can also take the gold back as a commodity rather than buy and transport goods. If he returns with the gold and the gold will buy him more goods back home than he took with him, he will have made a profit. He could also take a loss, but the option belonged to the trader and whether he returned with goods or coins he would be returning home with a commodity of intrinsic value.

Carrying gold and silver around everywhere you went did nothing but encourage thieves and robbers. Being good with a blade or a bow was important in those days. Somewhere along the line, businessmen, and or traders, learned that they could leave their money with the king in the land where they were doing business for safekeeping. Of course the king would put it in his vaults, and before long it usually became obvious that kings made the laws and were often little better than robbers and thieves in fine clothing. Then bankers showed up as third parties. Banks eventually gained the military or police security of the king and the confidence of the merchants and traders. A merchant could sign a piece of paper saying the bearer of the certificate could receive so much in gold upon demand from the bank in which the merchant had previously deposited gold; the bank was sponsored or protected by the government in the country where the merchant made the sale. The certificate often bore the name of the person to be paid as well as those of the person issuing the note and the bank. It was very much like writing a personal check. Sometimes these notes were backed by an individual, sometimes by a business, sometimes by royalty, or a kingdom, and sometimes by the bank itself. These arrangements were much more convenient than carrying around a lot of gold and silver.

Somewhere along the line, merchants and traders learned that these paper notes could be traded if the issuer had a good reputation. They became in effect a form of money. Sometimes the notes would trade hands many times and end up back in the country of origin where it was issued in the first place before it was ever cashed. It was really the beginning of commercial credit.

In the end the bills would trade hands, and one bank would end up with paper bills from another kingdom, while the bank in the other kingdom collected bills from the merchants in the other country. At the end of a given period of time, say one year, the two banks would tally the totals from the other country and exchange them one for one. If one bank was left with more bills after the exchange, the bank owing payment on the remaining bills would ship the amount of the untraded bills, in gold, to the other bank in exchange for the bills. This was the rise of the Gold Exchange Rate which is an outgrowth of the gold standard. Using notes for money also allowed banks to keep their gold in reserve in their vaults while the paper circulated.

Eventually, in the modern world, paper money and electronic transfers became king. When we buy goods from Japan, the companies in Japan that export the goods are paid in American dollars. Here I'm assuming the various individuals or companies in both countries are writing checks that will pass through their respective central bank. Unfortunately the Japanese firms can't use dollars in Japan. The same is true for goods we export to Japan. The firms in the United States are paid in yen. The yen and dollars pass through their respective central banks and the central banks credit the bank accounts of the firms in their countries with their country's currency. Firms in the United States would receive dollars, Japanese firms would receive yen, and the central banks would end up holding the other country's currency. Every so often, and it may happen daily, the Bank of Japan (Japan's central bank) and the Federal Reserve exchange currencies. Since it is usually just paper transactions and not actual currency that is exchanged, everything is done by wire transfers, and the banks just write off the same amount of money according to the current exchange rate. If one bank is left holding money that couldn't be written off, it is termed a trade deficit, which is owed to the bank that holds the excess currency from the other country. The money that can't be written off is not a debt. In this instance deficit refers to an imbalance in the trade denominated in the currency of the country with the smaller amount of trade.

The central bank of a country is really the bank that represents the government of the country in which it resides. The central bank will process money for individuals and businesses and pay them off, purchase the foreign currency in exchange for the local currency, which leaves the central bank holding the foreign currency. The central bank can then trade the currency with the issuing country for gold. In this day and age gold doesn't usually trade hands; the trade usually happens in bonds created by the debtor government. The bonds are traded in cash equivalent and of course the bonds can be redeemed with the issuing country in their currency. With two exceptions, holding bonds is the same thing as holding the other country's cash: the bonds bear interest which goes to the country holding the bond and the fluctuating value of the bonds in the market.

In the last number of paragraphs I have given the example of traders (businesses) selling goods in a foreign country and not bring a commodity (gold or something else) back with them to their homeland. Instead they bring back money in any of its forms. Since the traders are dealing with money issued by a specific country it requires that the money be exchanged, redeemed, with the government that issued it. This often requires a central bank to represent the government.

Here I have depicted foreign trade payments made by companies writing checks from their bank accounts and processing them through central banks. This can happen but is such a slow process it usually doesn't happen. What usually happens follows the same process except commercial banks usually deal with their counterparts in the other country directly or through the *foreign exchange market.* The foreign exchange market consists of several large entities that bring holders of foreign currencies together and they swap currencies and pay the exchange entity a small fee for the arrangements. In this case the holders of foreign currencies are usually large commercial banks or multinational corporations.

The creation of central banks and a foreign exchange market also created a dual banking system. One banking system was between nations with independent currencies and the other was within countries where one currency is traded for all domestic transactions. This has the effect of making the nations responsible for their own currencies and all exchanges between countries would take place through the central banks or the foreign exchange market. Originally the central banks or the government would store gold and hold it in reserve to pay for imbalances with other countries. This made it so banks didn't have to keep gold reserves. Today reserves are held in cash or in the other countries securities which in effect is the same as holding currency. There is even an informal currency exchange system known as "hawala" that avoids banks all together but most money goes through the central banks or the foreign exchange market and the informal exchange system is not where we want to go.

A trader or business always has the option of avoiding the central banks and foreign exchange market by buying other commodities in the foreign country and taking them home. By doing this the trader does not send money home and avoids having to exchange currencies. As an example if a Japanese car maker were to sell cars in our country they would most likely deposit the money in an American bank. If the car maker didn't wish to exchange our dollars for yen it could simply turn around and buy materials in the United States to ship home or invest the money in a local businesses or even securities. Securities can be bought anywhere and sold somewhere else. They are a truly global commodity.

In the example using checks and the central banks the money is easy to follow, as is where the money ends up. With lots of Banks and multinational firms swapping currencies in the foreign exchange market the money is much harder to follow, but the total deficit or surplus between countries would still be the same. It would just be held by many players rather than one. So I will use the central bank analogy for most of my explanations because it is simpler.

So far we have looked at the exchange of money and banks and central banks, but the one concept we have not looked at so far is the balance of trade. In the above example, if the Japanese car maker sells the cars for $100,000.00 and puts it in the bank and the next day buys $100,000.00 worth of materials and ships them home he has created $100,000.00 in sales (exports) in the United States and $100,000.00 in purchases (imports) to be shipped to Japan. The trade is balanced, exports equal imports. This is also true of the traders long ago who traded for gold, in coin or bullion, as a commodity with intrinsic value. In the same example from above if the Japanese car maker sends the money home rather than purchasing goods to ship back to Japan there will have been $100,000.00 in exports but no import of goods into Japan. Japan's central bank will purchase the dollars from the car manufacturer in exchange for Yen, Japanese currency. The central bank of Japan will then be left with $100,000.00 in US currency. Since there was not a corresponding purchase in the United States The central bank of Japan will now have $100,000.00 it can not swap in the foreign exchange market. At this point since cash doesn't make profits the central banks best option would be to buy US securities, which are denominated and will be paid off in dollars plus the securities pay interest. Later in this chapter we will look at the *balance of payments* which includes the purchase of foreign securities by central banks, commercial banks and others. I hope you now understand better the process of international trade and I would like to return, at this point, to some of the more historical aspects of the gold standard.

Today's financial world divorced itself from the gold standard that existed back around the time of World War I and the Great Depression. After World War II the Bretton Woods agreement made the US dollar king and kept it convertible to gold at a fixed price, which was similar to the gold standard but not quite. It was termed the Gold Bullion Standard where gold could be exchanged for dollars, on demand, at a fixed price. In the early 1970s, President Nixon ended the convertibility of dollars into gold, and the gold standard in all its forms was history.

Back when the gold standard was in force, if one country had a trade deficit, there came a point when the countries to which

Country A owed money demanded gold in return for the money that was left over after currencies were exchanged. Country A would pay in gold what it owed. Because a country's money was valued by the gold the country held in reserve, the transfer of gold would lower the value of Country A's currency in relation to the currency of the country receiving the gold. The country receiving the gold would find its currency going up in value in relation to Country A's currency. When Country A's currency dropped far enough in value in relation to the other country's currency, Country A's exports would became cheaper, while the other country's exports became more expensive. At some point the pendulum would swing, and Country A, which had the trade deficit, saw its goods decrease in price relative to the other country's currency, such that its exports increased to the point where Country A now started building a surplus, and gold started flowing back the other way. Eventually trade developed a sense of equilibrium, and gold stopped passing between countries in large quantities. But when the gold standard existed, gold was the great equalizer and tended to balance trade.

In reality the gold standard was never quite universal. Nations often tried to cheat so they didn't have to give up gold, and some countries were just too poverty ridden to have any gold to use. Eventually, as paper money became the medium of exchange, countries learned that they could just print money, which would eventually cause their currencies to go down in value in relation to other countries and thus increase their exports. In the short run, this helps exports; however, it is inflationary, and inflation creates winners and losers within the country's economy as well as the global economy. In modern times, with the rise of central banks, if the rulers of a country wanted, they could manipulate the value of money by having the central bank dabble, or cheat, in the gold or money market (which includes the foreign exchange market) as well as print money on the sly. Most countries that have open and transparent monetary policies and central banks that are independent of the political process usually don't cheat, and other countries know how and why they are dabbling in the markets. There are countries in which the central banks are under the influence of opaque political processes, and no one knows what is happening to their currency, much less why. This is why China has a currency that is almost useless in international markets. No one knows for sure what the governments monetary policy is or what the currency's real value is, and traders could get burned very quickly. Since no one really wants to deal or trade with such a currency, it is almost useless in international dealings.

While the gold standard was not perfect or universal, it was the best way ever devised to help bring balance to international trade between countries. There has been an effort to allow the free market to replace the gold standard. The free market for money could best be described as a country's allowing its currency to float in the money market or foreign exchange market. The value of a country's currency would thus be determined by supply and demand. Unfortunately most countries don't float their currencies; most use some kind of peg which ties their currency to another currency, basket of currencies or a commodity like gold or oil, so it too has not been a perfect balancing system for trade. Since the demise of the gold standard, there has been nothing in place to really balance trade between countries.

Here the important thing is not the trade or the exports and imports themselves but the balancing of trade itself. If the system is to be fair, there must be a universal system in place that will balance trade without killing trade. We have looked at gold as a medium of exchange in paying off the trade imbalances, but the world seems to have rejected the gold standard. We have looked at money and what part it plays in the balancing process and it just doesn't seem to work either.

So why is balance in trade so important? The main reason is that wealth is transferred from one country to another in the amount of the deficit or surplus. Let's take another look at central banks. When traders traded for goods to take back home with them there was no trade deficit. The exchange of wealth was immediate. In the example of the Japanese car manufacturer selling cars in our country, our central bank transfers the dollars to the Bank of Japan which in turn exchanges those dollars with yen that it gives to the auto maker. At this point the car manufacturer has been paid and received the exchange of wealth in his native currency. Now the Japanese central bank needs to do something with its excess holdings in dollars. It can keep the dollars as part of its reserve currency, which has many uses that I won't explain here, but if it holds the cash, the cash generates no income. On the other hand if it invests in US securities which are denominated in US dollars it in effect keeps the dollars and earns interest on the securities. The central bank of Japan needs to put those dollars to work so it can use those dollars in the United States to invest in businesses or stocks or even in US securities or it can exchange them in the foreign exchange market for a different currency. Down the road, if the bank invests in US securities and the securities are eventually redeemed, paid off in dollars, the Bank of Japan will once again have dollars plus the interest earned on those securities and can go out and buy the same amount of new securities. This scenario applies equally well to commercial banks as it does to central banks. In the end the Car manufacturer has received the transfer of wealth and the bank or banks are encouraged to buy US securities. Because there are lots of buyers for US securities, interest rates on securities remain low, which in turn does nothing to discourage the United States government from increasing its national debt

If one country runs a surplus with another country for a long time, it removes wealth from the deficit country. In ancient times the transfer was in gold; today the transfers are businesses or commodities or securities. If the deficit is too great, it can seriously damage the economy of the country running the deficit. In the past many third world countries have experienced this because they needed things that first world countries had for sale. If the poorer country paid for the goods in gold, it bled the poorer country of its wealth or production, especially if it received nothing of lasting value in return. On the other hand, if the two countries traded in equal amounts, exports and imports being in balance, the exchange of wealth was even. If both countries were to grow their exports and imports in the same proportion, there is no reason their trade could not grow and remain balanced at the same time well into the future. Both countries would benefit from the added trade. Such a system works between two countries, and in order for it to work in a world with many countries, all the countries would have to abide by the same procedures. For each country to remain stable and healthy, it would have to have as many imports as exports.

When it comes to balancing exports and imports on a worldwide basis, there are probably two things that are necessary. The first would be a uniform system of trade. Probably the most efficient system of trading would be a truly free trade system, a system where there are no tariffs, legal restrictions, goods subsidized by a particular nation, or barriers to impede the sale of goods and services within countries. Since free trade alone does not ensure balance between imports and exports, the second necessity would be a specific system that would bring imports and exports into alignment.

The World Trade Organization (WTO) was established and given the responsibility to bring uniformity to trade agreements. Member countries are supposed to abide by rules that will liberalize trade between member nations (free trade or as close to free trade as you can get). The WTO supervises and provides a framework for resolving conflicts of interest between member nations. All regulation and treaties with the WTO must be agreed to by all members, which has weakened the organization's ability to move into the future simply because it hasn't been able to get everyone to agree to the same thing. The WTO still hasn't been able to pass the Doha Round (a worldwide free trade treaty). While the WTO is trying to make trade more free, it does not have a mandate to balance trade between nations.

One of the few mechanisms that exist for balancing trade has been the tariff. The real problem with the tariff is that it is usually used as a means of protecting a specific product or industry or of punishing a country for its supposed marketing tactics. The textiles and agriculture industries have had the most protection over the centuries. More recently modern manufacturing and technology have also received protective tariffs on their industries and goods. As an example of tariffs, Japan has maintained a near 800% tariff on imported rice in order to encourage its citizens to produce its own rice. Japan does so because it considers Japanese rice production to be strategic to its national welfare and defense. Tariffs are generally instigated in order to protect or punish.

A third problem with tariffs is that the tariff is a tax, and the money from the tariff usually goes to the government, not to the industry or workers involved. The politicians get money for their pet projects, the industries get their protection, and it becomes self-perpetuating.

Modern times, with advances in communication and transportation and fast transfers of money around the world, have seen at least one innovation in balancing trade. The Japanese in the 1970s and early 1980s shipped so many cars and electronics to the United States that the trade deficit was way off-kilter. The imbalance was so great that the US government prepared to place huge tariffs on those goods. Then the Japanese decided to relocate much of their manufacturing to plants in the United States, so the labor costs and jobs stayed in the United States. Some parts needed for the goods were also made here. Thus the Japanese companies were able to lower their exports to our country and still make the profits. Countries must be willing to let their businesses transfer some of their operations to countries with which they are running large surpluses, or the balancing doesn't happen.

Going back to tariffs, if tariffs were used to encourage balance rather than to protect or punish, they might be more valuable than they traditionally have been. In order to make tariffs more helpful, we could do two things: first, place the tariff on all goods coming from a country, and second, make the tariff small and incremental. Making the tariff the same on all goods coming from a country would not be protectionist of a specific industry or product. At the same time, it would be seen as making the trade imbalance a national problem, not a business or industry problem. By making it a national problem rather than protecting any specific industry, the government has to get involved and hopefully set national policies that will promote free and balanced trade. As an example let's assume that the trade deficit with Japan were about 50%. In the real world, Japan and the United States have a significant amount of trade going both ways, and our deficit with Japan in 2010 was about 50%. In other words it exported nearly twice as many goods, on a dollar basis, to us as we did to them. In order to balance our trade in dollar amounts, our government would need to place, on average, a 50% tariff on all goods coming from Japan. On average this would raise the price of goods coming from Japan by 50%, which in all likelihood would terminate all trade with Japan.

There is, however, another alternative. Suppose we were to negotiate a trade agreement with Japan where either country having a trade deficit of more than 2% could impose a tariff on all goods coming from the other country of one-tenth of the total percentage of the deficit, and an additional one-tenth of the previous year's deficit every year thereafter until balance was achieved, or until a balance of less than 2% was reached. In the case of Japan, where we have a 50% trade deficit, we could impose a 5% tax on all goods coming from Japan for the next twelve months. A 5% tax wouldn't totally kill our trade with Japan, but it might be sufficient to reduce Japan's exports to us by enough that the trade deficit would disappear. For the sake of argument, let us say that it reduced the trade imbalance to 10%.

Next year we could up the tax by 10% of the new imbalance, or 10% of 10%, which amounts to a 1% tax increase, for a total tariff of 6%. This would happen every year until the trade imbalance was within 2% of balancing. On the other side of the coin, if after putting the 5% tariff in place the balance shifted by the end of the year, so Japan suddenly had a 10% trade deficit with the United States, Japan could ask us to remove 1% of our existing tariff, lowering the tariff to 4%, and lower the rate by another 10% every year until balance was achieved.

Because the tariff would be small and incremental, Japan would be able to plan and encourage Japanese firms to move production to the United States or to buy goods and commodities from the United States to cut our trade balance while maintaining their output. They could also seek ways to encourage imports from the United States in areas for goods that the Japanese need so as to increase our trade with Japan while maintaining its level of exports to the United States. If the trade agreement also included free trade arrangements, as balance was achieved, the emphasis would be on building and equalizing trade rather than protectionism or punishment. There would be no limit to trade as long as both countries tried to stimulate trade in a balanced way. It would be a win-win situation for both countries.

At this point it might be of interest to you to know what some of our other trade imbalances were in 2010 according to the US Census Bureau.

Country	Approximate Deficit (%)
Britain	3%
Canada	10% (Canada was our #1 trading partner in 2010)
South Korea	20%
Mexico	25% (Mexico was our #3 trading partner in 2010)
Germany	30%
Japan	50%
China	70% (China was our #2 trading partner in 2010)

In the above-cited countries, with Britain, assuming the example I gave, a tariff in 2011 would only need to be around

0.3% to start balancing the trade deficit, whereas with China it would need to be around 7%.

I mentioned earlier that the revenue from tariffs goes to the government. It would be better if the tariff money was used for things directly related to commerce. Using the revenue to scan imports for security reasons or for contraband, which is important to our national security and to trade in general, would be a good place to use the money. This would necessitate investment in equipment and programs at major ports. Another good place to use the money would be in job training and placement. In the free market, especially where free trade and the global economy are concerned, many workers are displaced as industries change. It would be nice if there were funding that could be added to corporate funds to help upgrade the skills of displaced workers as well as a means to help them find new employment.

In the real world, there is not just a trade surplus or deficit in the trade of goods; there is also money exchanged for purchases of services and capital movement between countries. The balances of trade, service, and capital are said to make up the *balance of trade,* which is accompanied by a *balance of payments statement*. The *balance of payments* is always in balance because of the securities and financial transactions that pass between the countries. These payment transfers are considered inflows that balance the outflow of cash to the exporters.

Most economists say that the trade deficit is not a bad thing because the sale of securities (debt instruments) to foreign interests brings the money back, thus balancing out the flow of money. The economists seem to have the same disease that most Americans have. They think that money coming in from debt is income, and it is not. The money I spend when I use my credit card is not income. It is cash flow from a debt I have created.

The fact of the matter is that the *balance of payments statement* is a cash flow statement that happens to balance and not a balance sheet. There is money coming in from the securities, but it is money brought back to our country as a long-term IOU that bears interest that our children or grandchildren will have to repay, which will create a loss of wealth for our country. Too many people in this world treat money from the creation of debt as if it were income, and it is a disease that we need to eradicate. Eradication of a particular human behavior may not be what we are really after, but people need to be taught and expected to know that money from debt is definitely not income. The exchange of debt as a balancing mechanism between countries may balance the payments between countries, but it also affects the value of a county's currency. Like gold flowing from one country to another, the transfer of wealth should devalue the currency of the country that has the deficit and make the value of the currency from the country with the surplus go up. This would cause the balance of trade between the countries to change and come back into balance. However, countries can manipulate their currencies and cheat, or in some cases one country's currency can be the "international darling" in such a way that it doesn't have to pay the price or consequences of its deficit or surplus. Debt as a means of balance hasn't worked very well. The free market hasn't done a very good job of balancing trade either.

One can ask at this point, what does the trade deficit have to do with the multiplier effect of money or banking? Perhaps the best answer to this question would be to say, nothing directly. If the trade deficit really is a transfer of wealth, then we can ask, where is this wealth coming from as it departs the country? Are the imports bringing goods into the country that will be used in businesses or industry to create more jobs, exports, and wealth?

If a country is producing a lot of wealth, it can probably afford to spread some of that wealth around. But what if the imports are solely for consumption—things like jewelry, food, clothes, or personal transportation? Such personal consumption is often financed by consumers who are accumulating personal debt. And debt is always a part of the money supply, which of course involves the very role of banks. If the debt used to finance those imports is personal and short-term it creates volatility for the currency, which is what some of the previous chapters covered. Banks invariably get involved with the transfer of debt between nations. This builds wealth for the bank and expands the money supply, which involves the multiplier effect.

In the end wealth is what gives a nation the ability to be productive and lead in research and development. If the balance of trade transfers too much wealth out of a country, it can destroy the productivity and economy of that country, and for that reason the balancing of trade is important not only to us but to our posterity.

History is not just about dates and events.
In reality history is about people and how events affected their lives
and how they dealt and coped with those events.
It is also about how human beings in many cases created
or changed the events themselves!
Without the human element, history has
no meaning or relevance to other humans.

FINANCIAL HISTORY
(As I Have Seen It)

I first started noticing finance and monetary policy while I was serving on a mission for my church in Chile around 1970. The Chilean government was printing money, and inflation was somewhere around 20–30% per year. I had an allotted amount of money coming to me every month from my parents, and every month I would go to the bank and cash my check, which was made out in US dollars. Every month the number of escudos (Chilean currency) I received in exchange went up. In effect my expenses kept going down in relation to the money I received, and I had more and more money left over at the end of each month. It was great; I wish life were like that today. This was my first real life experience with inflation.

When I got back home, I immediately returned to college. A few years later, I got married, and then came the Arab Oil Embargo, and gasoline doubled in price. At the same time, there was a thing called the inflation spiral. I didn't understand the inflation spiral at the time. I was an undergraduate in business, but there was no mention of how the inflation spiral worked, only that it existed. My wife and I looked at home prices and started dreaming of someday buying a home. Costs of homes were going up, and so were interest rates. It wasn't until later that I figured out what the inflation spiral was all about.

Back in the 1960s, it was illegal for individuals or entities outside the United States to purchase US securities. The argument was that the United States should be indebted only to its own people. It was an issue of national security. The Federal Reserve would sell US securities only to American concerns. At the same time, the United States was engaged in a conflict in Southeast Asia, which kept escalating but never quite became a legitimate war. Unfortunately, declared or undeclared, the Vietnam War took its toll in fortune as well as blood. The federal government found its expenditures greater than its income and did the only thing it could do: go into debt. The debt was significant. The laws of supply and demand are valid not only for goods and services, but also for labor and capital. Capital is defined as the money in the economy that is available to be loaned out or otherwise invested. As the government could only borrow money from institutions and individuals in the United States, it was taking all the surplus capital out of the US markets. Because capital was scarce, the price of capital went up. Capital is really money, and the price of money is the interest rate you pay when you borrow it for your own use. At the same time, the Federal Reserve Board was pursuing a policy that would maintain interest rates at a low rate. Credit Unions and savings and loans were highly regulated, this was a carryover from the Great Depression, and they could charge only so much interest on loans to homeowners, among many other rules. As a result of all of the above, the Federal Reserve Board had reason to target interest rates and tried desperately to keep them down. The way to keep interest rates down is to increase the amount of money in the economy, as the supply goes up, there is more than enough to meet demand, so the interest rates drop or stay the same. Increasing the money supply is a fanciful way of saying that the government is printing money.

Of course the government wasn't printing money; it was merely letting the Federal Reserve Board buy more bonds in the bond market in an effort to increase the money supply in the market so the government could borrow the new capital out of the market to pay its bills. While this is basically the same thing as printing money, it sounds a whole lot better than saying the government is printing money so it could pay its bills. Because the Federal Reserve Board was making a serious effort to keep a lot of money in the economy, the supply of money was good, and interest rates accordingly remained low. Unfortunately increasing the money supply has the same effect on the value of money as does printing money. As a consequence the price of money eventually started inflating, and interest went up. The banks, realizing that their money, which they were loaning out, was losing its value, had to do something to compensate for the loss. (The principal of a loan would lose its value over the course of the years due to inflation). If a bank loaned you $100,000 for a home, and you paid it off over thirty years, and the inflation rate over those thirty years was 100%, then the house would now be worth $200,000. The bank would have been paid back $100,000 plus interest, but the $100,000 would now only buy half the same house as it did thirty years ago. (The bank lost 50% of the purchasing power of its money over those thirty years.) The only thing a bank can really do in this situation is to raise the interest rate to a level where the interest will make up for the loss of value due to inflation.

In order to compensate for inflation banks tried to go to interest rates that would change with inflation, or adjustable interest rates as they were often called. Raising the interest rate on money in this fashion is a lot like the cost of living increase that adjusts fixed pensions, like social security, so they rise in dollar amounts during times of inflation. Watching the banks raise interest rates to make up for inflation, of course, inspired the Federal Reserve Board to add more money to the pot and drive the interest rates back down again. Eventually banks and investors realized that interest rates had to go up even if the supply of money was good because the total quantity of money was going up all the time, causing inflation. It became a spiral; every time the Federal Reserve Board injected more money into the economy, the interest rates would dip down and then go up even more, and the Federal Reserve Board would pump more money into the economy in order to bring the interest rates back down, only to see the banks and investors raise the cost of borrowing money again. Interest rates were in an upward spiral. In the late sixties or early seventies, the increase in the money supply reached its climax, with the Federal Reserve Board increasing the money supply by over 10% per year. Annual increases in the money supply are compounded, and if you compound the yearly increases over a ten-year period of time in the sixties and early seventies, the Federal Reserve Board probably increased the money supply by well over 100%.

In 1973 I was a newlywed, and my wife and I started looking at the possibility of someday buying a home. Inflation was making the cost of houses go up every year, and it looked like inflation would go on forever. Interest rates were also climbing, and it was pushing the possibility of buying a home out of the reach of more and more people. And then came the Arab Oil Embargo. The price of gasoline doubled. Times were crazy. The cost of everything was going up and out of sight. During this time I was working in the construction industry, trying to support my family and go to school. With the cost of housing going up, the housing industry was doing everything it could to get people to continue buying houses. During the rest of the seventies, the construction industry was in turmoil but getting by.

Then came 1979. I was still in the construction industry, working on a framing crew building houses. The Federal Reserve Board had had enough of the inflation spiral. The Federal Reserve Board found itself between a rock and a hard spot with no way to turn. Increasing the money supply only increased the interest rates, and the government was still borrowing money. So the Federal Reserve Board decided to change its policy. It changed its policy from targeting interest rates to curbing (targeting) inflation. This meant the Federal Reserve Board would no longer pump money into the economy in huge amounts to keep interest rates low. When the Federal Reserve Board stopped pumping money into the market, the government, in order to pay its bills, quickly borrowed all the capital out of the money market. Supply and demand kicked in, and with very little money left in the market and the federal government still borrowing money, interest rates went out of sight. The prime rate on interest got up around 20% very quickly. The construction industry went into a slide. No one could afford a home, contractors that were speculating went under, and banks couldn't sell foreclosed homes. Everyone in the industry was looking for work wherever they could find it. We were headed into a major recession.

About this time Congress started realizing it needed to keep the electorate happy and decided to do something about the situation. Congress passed legislation that deregulated much of the financial industry. Three changes in particular that Congress made were, to allow savings and loans to use the multiplier effect, allow them to use the going interest rate on home loans, and allow special tax exemptions for limited partnerships in the commercial construction industry.

Savings and loans had never been able to loan money that they did not have. Before this time they depended solely on savings deposited, with those cash savings being used to finance homes and cars. In other words the savings and loans could only loan out the cash they had on hand and nothing more. The savings and loans had also had regulations limiting the interest they could charge on loans that they made. They were going bankrupt because of the difference in the two interest rates. They had to pay the high interest rate to keep people saving at their institutions, yet they could not place high interest rates on loans in order to make the money to pay the high interest to the savers. All of a sudden things had changed with the new laws. The savings and loans were sitting on all this cash from the savers and could now use the cash as reserve requirements and make loans at an unprecedented rate. At the same time, the savings and loans could also use their cash in limited partnerships with commercial contractors and get the tax breaks as well as profits. The managers of the savings and loans had never had it so good. They started increasing their salaries and having parties and living the good life. They were making money and creating wealth, and times were great.

Then in the mid-eighties, the oil industry succumbed to the glut of oil production, and the price of petroleum products plummeted. The Arab Oil Embargo had spurred the exploration and development of new sources of crude oil. The price of oil during the seventies had remained fairly high, and oil companies were exploring and bringing new oil into production, causing a glut of oil on the market. Texas, Oklahoma, Louisiana, and other states that were heavily involved in the oil industry suddenly found oil companies laying off employees and cutting off new exploration. Many people couldn't afford the payments on their homes, and suddenly the savings and loan industry was hit with a huge number of foreclosures. It was quickly apparent that the savings and loans had overstretched their financial abilities. It also became apparent that the limited partnerships, in their desire to build and avoid taxes, had built far more offices and commercial buildings than the market could absorb. The savings and loan industry went belly-up, and we were headed into a recession once more.

The Federal Savings and Loan Insurance Corporation (FSLIC) bailed out the depositors at the savings and loans, and the Federal Reserve Board and other agencies helped wind down the bad savings and loans. Other banks also went down in the recession. Congressmen and other people looking at the savings and loans in particular were asking where all the money had gone and blaming managers for living and partying with all the money. I hope you will understand that the money was created out of thin air and could disappear just as easily. It is the nature of the business. The politicians didn't get the idea that the money never really existed in the first place. It was on the books as being there, but when the loans went bad, the money was just gone.

The government and the regulators did one thing that turned out to be a good deal. They created a temporary organization called the Resolution Trust Corporation (RTC), which would take all the distressed properties from the savings and loans as well as banks and auction or sell them to investors and the public in an effort to recover as much of the money that had been lost as possible. Creating money out of thin air also creates mortgages and liens on property, and the money created is tied up in the market value of the assets involved. The RTC was able to sell most of the properties and make something like seventy cents on the dollar of the original properties' values. Losses were held to around 30%. And then the RTC disappeared. If it hadn't been for the FSLIC and the other regulatory agencies involved, we might well have ended up in a depression in the mid-eighties.

Coming out of the eighties, the United States was in the throes of two of the most sweeping transformations the world has ever seen. One was technological, the other political, but they both had huge effects on our economy. One was the advent of the personal computer and the Internet. During the 1990s the United States saw its economy expand at an unprecedented rate. Hundreds of thousands of jobs were created. The economy expanded, expansive monetary policy was absorbed by the economy, and times were great. Expansive money supplies meant that the Federal Reserve Board was expanding the money supply, but at the same time the economy was growing so fast that the expansion of the money supply didn't cause inflation. With the expansion of the economy, the economy needed the infusion of money to keep the dollar from deflating, which would have caused a recession. Remember deflation causes the value of money to go up, and if the value of money goes up, the price of everything, including labor, comes down, which is deflation.

At the same time, a problem arose called Y2K (year two thousand). It was predicted that in the year 2000 we would see all the computers shut down because of a glitch in their dating systems. All of a sudden there weren't enough programmers to handle rewriting computer dating programs. Jobs were expanding like crazy. Then there was the dot-com bubble, and it burst. A lot of jobs were lost in the bust. But many unemployed individuals with computer skills moved into jobs in the Y2K arena, and the recession wasn't all that bad. Y2K came and went, and with it quite a few jobs, but it wasn't that bad for the economy in general.

The second major change to affect the 1990's was the end of the Cold War. The Berlin Wall came down, and communism has nearly become an historical note. With the fall of the USSR, trade expanded, and the global economy truly became global. Finance also went global. This all happened at the same time as the rise of computers and the Internet.

One minor and one major event at the turn of the century also had an effect on the banking industry in the US that you might be interested in. One was the anthrax bacteria scare in 2001. When anthrax powder was found in the mail, sent to government officials, the postal system was temporarily shut down on a good portion of the East Coast for investigation and decontamination. Many people sent their home loan payments, credit card payments, and utility payments through the mail, to mention a few. The great juggling act at the banks found itself greatly disrupted. Once again the Federal Reserve did its job and took care of the banks' cash needs until everything ran smoothly again. Because of the Federal Reserve's actions, in most cases banks were able to be understanding with their customers and not charge late fees. It turned out to be a very minor financial incident as far as the public was concerned. The other incident was the 9/11 attacks on the World Trade Center and the Pentagon. Once again it threw the great juggling act into disarray. Again the Federal Reserve stepped in and made sure things moved almost seamlessly into the future. Just before these two incidents happened, the Federal Reserve Bank branch here in Kansas City had made it a policy to get all the banks in its district to sign paperwork and have all the legal necessities in place so that if there was a financial disruption the Federal Reserve Bank of Kansas City could pump money into the banks of the district on a moments notice without further red tape. The Federal Reserve really is a valuable institution. It provides the means of stability during many crises that most of the public may not even be aware of.

During the 1970s President Nixon got rid of the convertibility of the dollar to gold and the remnants of the gold standard with it. Later the sale of US securities was opened to all comers. It no longer mattered who bought the securities; even foreign governments could now buy them. This took a lot of pressure off the capital market in our country and helped keep interest rates down.

At this point I need to take you down another path and show you a different banking world than the one I have presented. It runs parallel to the history I have described, so its time frame will overlap.

After World War II, the financial world went through some real changes with the Bretton Woods agreement. Later, in the 1950s, the Colonial Era came to an end, and there were many newly independent countries. Still later, in the 1970s, the dollar's convertibility to gold was terminated. The financial world was changing. Former colonies never had to worry about the financing of their governments; it was taken care of by their colonial masters. Financing new governments was a huge marketplace for loans. New countries suddenly had independence and wanted everything all the colonial masters of the world had.

Banks began making loans to these and other third world countries. The banks seemed to be of the opinion that these countries would be stable and repay their debts on time. Unfortunately things didn't work out that way. There came a time when Latin American countries went into default in droves. Then there was the Asian financial crisis, and many Asian countries found themselves overextended. Most of these countries had little experience in international finance, and in many cases runaway corruption in the government was the root cause of their financial problems. It all created financial turmoil, and that turmoil was somewhere other than here in the United States, so most Americans didn't pay much attention to what was going on. I had become interested in the International Monetary Fund (IMF) and its involvement in the resolution of the problem on a country-by-country basis.

There is also something called offshore banking and banking through foreign branches of US banks. Offshore banks are in places that are often exotic, where the government has little or no regulation of the banking industry. Foreign branches of US banks could often operate under the regulations of the countries where the branches were located, rather than under US regulations.

Offshore banking offers three attractive services. The first is that offshore banks operate with little or no regulation. This means they may have little or no reserve requirements or equity ratio to meet. Without such restrictions offshore banks could take huge risks and make lots of money. In doing so they were willing to share the profits with depositors by offering significantly higher returns on depositors' money than depositors could get in their own countries. Of course risks were high, and some banks failed, but if you picked a reputable, well-established bank, things were usually good. The second service offered was privacy. An offshore bank was supposed to be a secret place to hide your money. If you open an account and put something in it the account, who owned it, how much was in it, and how much you made on your money ceased to exist. It was like a black hole. Swiss banks were considered to be offshore, and they had impeccable credibility. They were the ultimate black hole in the financial industry in part because the Swiss government wanted it to be that way.

The third attractive offer of off-shore banks was that the countries in which they resided charged little or no taxes on the income generated or interest received by account holders. They were tax havens and attracted the money of the rich and well-connected that did not want to pay taxes.

Branch banks in other countries, particularly if the country was lax on regulation, had the ability to act in some ways like off shore banks. Usually they weren't as private as true offshore banks, but they usually had lower reserve and equity requirements, which meant they were great profit centers for the main bank as well as account holders.

Because of the privacy aspect of offshore banking, the banks attracted many covert deposits. Drug dealers, terrorist organizations, dictators, tax evaders, and mafia were very interested in the banks' services. Of course these banks also had legitimate dealings with regulated financial institutions around the world and had the ability to launder money for such groups, in a very private way.

Offshore banks were involved in financing new countries and third world countries because both needed money and usually had to pay higher interest rates to get loans and deposits. Of course if the bank had no reserve requirement, it could make the loans without putting any of its own money in reserve, and for those banks the great juggling act went out of sight. But most dictators siphoned off a lot of the borrowed money into their bank accounts. If the bank loaning the money could get the dictator and his cronies to put the filched money back into accounts with the off shore bank, read black holes, the money never went anywhere in the end, and profit for the bank went up, while the country kept paying interest on money that was in the possession of the bank. Of course, down the road ten years, the government could no longer afford to make interest and principal payments, so the banks restructured the loans, drawing out payments and/or decreasing the amount of interest paid, but it still continued to make interest and principal on money that was in the bank. Again some loans went belly-up or had some of the principal written off, and some of the banks had to take partial losses, but as long as they could continue to get the country to make payments, times were good.

During the eighties and nineties, many countries went through borrowing binges and defaults or restructuring. I remember wondering why anyone would make a loan to such countries and thinking the banks had to be crazy, but now understand why they did it.

Organizations like the IRS, FBI, CIA, and DEA have always wanted to know who has accounts in offshore banks, how much money is in them, and where that money came from. Because the offshore banks operate in other countries, there is no legal remedy for finding out such information. With the 9-11 attacks and the declaration of the War on Terror, many countries have banded together to obtain leverage over the offshore banks. To a great extent, they have been successful. Today offshore banks will hand out a great deal more information to such organizations. I doubt seriously that the banks' books are open to such organizations, but they have started cooperating in certain cases. Even Swiss banks have opened up a crack, but it has taken a concerted and coordinated effort on the part of many countries to gain what little they have been able to.

At this point I hope you have been entertained by my parallel history and as a result understand a little more about offshore banking as well as foreign branch operations of major banks. So let's now return to the other part of history as I have seen it.

With the end of Maoist rule in China and a change in Indian economic policy, the seventies, eighties, and nineties saw economic changes on the Asian continent, and we have seen Asia rise as one of the world's great trading and economic arenas. China, with its export-oriented economy and political intervention against imports and competition from abroad, has helped the United States' foreign trade deficit climb to over $800 billion per year in 2007. At the same time, the United States has never developed the ability to deal with trade imbalances since the gold standard was removed as a means of paying off trade imbalances.

Of course the first decade of the new century was the age of globalization. East and South Asia were growing leaps and bounds. Latin America was beginning to get its act together, and it seemed like nothing would get in the way of continued global growth. Hubris set in in the commercial banking and financial industries. Risk seemed to have been tamed, swept aside by economics, creative finance, and the free market. Yet problems lurked underneath the surface. The housing bubble in the United States eventually burst, and with it came down many of the risky financial ventures that had been created. Counterbalancing all of this has been the intervention of central banks and governments.

In 2007 the world was turned upside down. Free markets were revealed to be not nearly as free as supposed. Government intervention and regulation were suddenly supreme. Financial institutions have been increasingly blamed for the problems and misery that we face. The truth probably lies in a combination of the greed of banks and the citizens, businesses, and governments thinking they could go into endless debt with impunity.

The free market seems to be an eternal principle. Any nation over the course of history that has sought to fight the free market has either eventually been crushed by the forces of the free market or left to suffer under the bondage of some form of economic slavery. The free market of necessity includes goods, services, labor, and capital. Some of the all-important supports of the free market are freedom of information, press, and speech, and freedom of movement, commerce, money, and migration. Last but not least among the supports of the free market is government regulation.

Hubris, greed, and dishonesty in their many forms are human qualities. They are not a part of the free market but rather brought to the market by the intents and actions of participants in the market. Regulation on the actions of the individuals and the entities who trade within the market is just as important to the proper function of the market as the need for the government to stay out of the market itself. No one has ever found anything that can replace the free market for getting things done in the best possible and fairest way. No one has ever found humans to be without greed, pride, and a desire to advance themselves at the expense of others. The only medium that seems to help is to regulate individual activities in the market while leaving the market itself free to do its thing. There are individuals and groups who believe that for the market to be free it must exist without regulation. That is the equivalent of saying a free society can exist only where there are no laws to govern the people. Unfortunately anarchy is not a good way for society to rule people or the marketplace.

My account of history has brought us up fairly close to the financial crisis of 2007. Of course it is not a complete history, and recent history is something all of us have experienced. Hopefully this book will help you understand some of it.

History is fascinating, and each individual may see it a little differently, for we each have differing interests as well as histories of our own. As I look at the world, as I write today, many of the banks and governments in Europe and the euro itself are on the verge of collapse. The Middle East is in the throes of huge changes. Energy supplies are changing in ways we didn't imagine. The United States is in political gridlock. History is in the making, and we are in the thick of it all, whether we like it or not. The truth is we will see history unfold. Let's hope we can see it for what it is and move forward in an undeterred manner, creating the economy and institutions that will bring about a brighter future. Understanding the creation of money through the multiplier effect of money is an important key to understanding not only our economy but also the global economy. And of course our economies are subject to economic principles, and economic principles and economies are really about our jobs, private enterprise, and government policy. For these reasons I hope you have understood what I have written and find it of value.

The act of reading can be solely for entertainment.
However, if our minds and hearts are not invigorated,
imbued with a desire to be better,
achieve more,
or simply grateful for the extent and depth of our own lives,
regardless of what our lives might be,
we are but fools!

CONCLUSION

We live in a world where life itself, as well as health, circumstance, wealth, and good fortune can be quite ephemeral. The opposite of risk is security. Security depends upon life, health, circumstance, wealth, and good fortune, all of which are often nothing more than chimeras.

Of course we all seek security, and the irony of it all is that in doing so, we must take risks. We have to stretch out our necks and do something. The fact that we must take risks does not mean that we cannot calculate and weigh those risks against the rewards and make informed decisions, but we cannot have security without taking risks.

Throughout this book the major objective of the multiplier effect of money has been portrayed as the creation of debt. Debt creates risk as well as wealth, and that risk probably goes up exponentially as debt approaches and then exceeds the value of one's assets. When debts go beyond the value of one's underlying assets, one's ability to produce income is the only thing sustaining the house of cards which supports our financial security.

There are at least two major problems with debt. First, the maintenance, payment toward debt, is always accomplished through one's income. The maintenance or servicing of debt limits the freedom of the individual who is indebted. If you lose your job you must find another fairly quickly, or you may be in financial trouble. If you have heavy debts or are upside down on a loan, you lose not only your freedom to take a little time to find another job, but you also can't afford to take a job that does not offer at least as much as you were making before. This also means you are not free to move if your employment moves, or, if you lose your employment, you cannot move to another market because you can't take the loss brought on by the sale of your home. If you are upside down on payments for a home, vehicle, or business, you can't sell them without taking a loss. Being in such a position changes your options and possibilities under adverse conditions.

Debt always limits one's freedom, and in the end it can totally enslave you. Being totally free from debt brings freedom. And while it may seem ironic, freedom brings security. We simply cannot have security without freedom. I believe this to be a universal truth, so let me write it again: ***you cannot have security without freedom, and you cannot have freedom without taking risks.*** It is equally true to say ***"freedom always has a price."*** If you want to secure your wealth, you must take risks or inherit it. If you want to secure your political freedom, you must share it with others, which will require you to give up some of your own freedom. If you want to secure an income during retirement, you must sacrifice income over a lifetime either to investment or taxes. If through investments, you take your security into your own hands and the hands of the market. If through taxes, you place yourself in the hands of the government, politicians, and the ever-changing political winds.

In the end if you have no debt in your personal finances, you will have more freedom and flexibility when it comes to making choices. Having no debt is an enviable position to be in and one that will help guarantee your security. Being debt free in our personal lives where possible is one of our best choices. So in all probability we should avoid debt like we would the plague. This may fly in the face of current economic theory, but, if you are interested in freedom of choice, it is one of the best decisions anyone can make on an individual basis.

The second problem is derived from the fact that many people treat debt as if it were income.. *Debt is not income!* Hopefully that sounds obvious, but too many people act as if debt is a means of income. This is true not only for individuals, but also for businesses and governments. If any one of the three has a debt burden that it cannot meet with current income, it is in trouble. *If individuals, businesses or governments wish to have security, they must seek to keep themselves out of debt. There are no exceptions, only delusions! Sometimes debt is necessary or unavoidable, but if individuals, businesses or governments do not have a plan in place to repay the debt, and actually put the plan into effect, they will see their debts increase and their freedom and security dissipate.*

This brings us to the end, and in the end I believe we would all like to be better off than when we started, or perhaps just better off than where we are now. I hope this book has added to your knowledge and as well, given you an understanding of things that can perhaps bring you greater freedom and security.

www.ingramcontent.com/pod-product-compliance
Lightning Source LLC
Chambersburg PA
CBHW071425170526
45165CB00001B/396